Hypothermia

The Silent Killer

Lyn Thompson

Detselig Enterprises Ltd.
Calgary, Alberta

© 1989 by **Lyn Thompson**

Calgary, Alberta

Canadian Cataloguing in Publication Data

Thompson, Lyn.
  Hypothermia : the silent killer

  ISBN 0-920490-90-5

  1. Hypothermia.   2. Outdoor recreation –
Safety measures.   I. Title.
  RC88.5.T46 1989   616.9'89   C89-091207-6

Detselig Enterprises Limited
P.O. Box G 399
Calgary, Alberta T3A 2G3

Printed in Canada   SAN 115-0324   ISBN 0-920490-90-5

*This book is dedicated to my husband
and four sons who, each in his own unique way,
contributed to the origin of this book.*

Foreword

Hypothermia is a medical problem characterized by its insidious onset, and often deadly outcome. Nevertheless, with reasonable knowledge, people most likely to encounter this illness can either prevent it or arrest it before major consequences occur.

Lyn Thompson has captured the essence of understanding and preventing hypothermia in this book. The short story describing a recreational outdoor adventure – the setting in which hypothermia is often experienced, enhanced my motivation to read *Hypothermia: The Silent Killer*. The story is captivating, yet, serves only as a precursor to well-researched and well-written information on the prevention and the management of hypothermia in the field.

All who read this book will derive important information on hypothermia from it, and it should be on the required reading list of every person who wishes to tackle the great outdoors.

G. Powell
M.D., F.R.C.P.C.
Chief, Division of Emergency Medicine
Foothills Hospital

A Disclaimer

This book is a very concise source of information on hypothermia and as such does not attempt to completely cover this complex subject. Although every attempt has been made to present all sides of the subject, the brevity of presentation has precluded discursive attention to detail.

The illness hypothermia may exhibit many variables unique to the physiology of each individual and their particular reaction to cold. Environmental temperature and topography, the number of people in the group and the group's distance from civilization, coupled with their degree of exhaustion, all present variables with which to be contended and judged for pertinence to the situation. These many variables, both physiological and physical, necessitate that neither the author nor the publisher accept any legal or moral responsibility, nor any liability, for applications of information found in this book, or for actions taken in a hypothermic situation. This book is not intended to be a substitute for your physician's advice.

Contents

Illustrations

Preface

Hypothermia is an illness that overtakes the human body when outer cold cools the body faster than the body can produce heat to stay warm. Medically, the definition of hypothermia is the progressive collapse of the human body, both physically and mentally, as the temperature of the body inner core decreases to approximately 35.5 °C and lower.

Hypothermia has only been studied closely as a medical illness in the last twenty-five years. Prior to that it was known as exposure, and doctors didn't fully understand the body defense mechanisms against cold. It is still not fully understood, but researchers are actively testing new theories and treatments, protective clothing and equipment every day; in search of new information and improved medical treatment.

Generally, hypothermia can be divided into three categories, depending on the cause of the illness and the length of time needed for the onset of its symptoms. The onset of chronic hypothermia is slow, as the name implies. Hypothermia due to exhaustion and environmental cold comes on in a matter of hours, while the hypothermia of accidental immersion happens within minutes of contact with cold water. Just as the body responds to these three stimuli in different although related ways, so does the medical treatment vary in each case. The information in this book will address the form of hypothermia encountered with cold environmental temperatures.

Death due to cold temperatures is common in everyday life. It affects the very young and the elderly suffering from cold housing conditions and malnutrition. Outside workers subjected to extreme cold, such as workers on ships or oil rigs and winter joggers, suffer in varying degrees. Persons with illnesses that affect their ability to stay warm, including alcohol and drug abusers, are predisposed to hypothermia. People living in rural areas and and those involved in outdoor sports perish in the wilderness when they are unable to return to civilization to get warm. Victims of an unexpected outdoor emergency, through ignorance of hypothermia, find themselves unprepared and defenseless against the cold. Can you afford to be unprepared?

The outdoor emergency, with hypothermia as a secondary but more alarming problem, is the most common cause of hypothermia. An unforeseen emergency such as vehicle breakdown, getting lost, or running into bad weather makes a prime setting for hypothermia. Once the emergency is upon you, it is too late to think about what you should have done to be prepared. You must learn about and plan against hypothermia before you are confronted with it.

The majority of hypothermia cases develop between the temperature range of 0°C to 10°C (32°F to 50°F). People don't think of these temperatures as being dangerous and fail to take precautions against the cold. Knowing about hypothermia *before* it threatens may save your life and the lives of your friends.

Be safe – think hypothermia.

Acknowledgements

My long association with the outdoor world of Guiding and Scouting and the many courses taken under their auspices, coupled with a hypothermic situation involving one of my family, initiated the study that has gone into this work. Acknowledgements would not be complete without expressing my appreciation to the many people involved in this history.

I would like to thank those who read the first draft of the book and offered me helpful opinions and encouragement: Gabriela Samuels, Cliff Gundry-White, Dr. Jack Ibberson, Bob Schwartzenberger and Dean Desireau. Their expertise in education, medicine and outdoorsmanship was invaluable.

Finally, I wish to thank Dr. Greg Powell, Chief of Emergency Medicine, Foothills Hospital. His intimate knowlege of the study of hypothermia, continued support and medical opinions throughout the final drafts of this book allow me, and ultimately you, the reader, to have confidence in the medical accuracy of this book.

Detselig Enterprises Ltd. appreciates the financial assistance for its 1989 publishing program from

Alberta Foundation for the Literary Arts
Canada Council
Department of Communications
Alberta Culture

Part A
The Silent Killer - A Story

The life of a frontiersman is a grand life, but to live it, you must prepare yourself in advance for difficulties that may arise.

Lord Baden-Powell of Gilwell
Founder of the Boy Scout Movement
(1857-1941)

The adventure story you are about to read is based on a true experience concerning two healthy, strong young men who could have died on their hectic canoe trip. The killer would have been hypothermia. Fortunately, one of the youths had been warned of this illness and recognized that he must try to prevent it without waiting to see if it would overtake him and his friend.

This story is your warning. It is up to you to learn what hypothermia is all about before you are confronted with it. Without this knowledge it might be your life that will be lost in the event of a similar emergency.

Read this book and then think back over this story. Try to pick out the things that helped the situation, and where mistakes were made. With your new knowledge, consider what you would have done if you were in a similar situation.

1

The Silent Killer

Wilderness! Miles and miles of wilderness! Even the word sounds unpredictable thought Greg as he sat with his heels digging into the pebbled beach, his back against a gnarled tree. He wondered why a city kid like him would find the wilderness so magical. Beauty? Adventure? Danger? All true, he mused as he toyed with the significance of each word and considered the scene before him.

A warm breeze ruffled the bulrushes growing in the shallows, birds whistled and the sun hung in the evening sky. He felt at peace. His gaze spread to the bend in the river where mountain water rippled on its way to the prairies. The distant hills and sky blended to form a backdrop for the willows and dogwood growing along the far bank.

This was Greg's first summer job away from home. It had brought him to the oil fields of Swan Hills, Alberta. The work camp's portable trailers nestled among the trees along the Freeman River, and all around, the tracts of spruce forest filled the horizon. The workers would venture into the forest on their days off and by midsummer they had climbed every height and explored each glistening lake. When no one was available for a ramble, Greg would go down to the river. It wasn't that far from the bunkhouse and it was a great spot for fishing.

"Hey Greg! Come and have a beer with the new guy who

5

just arrived! We're having our usual welcome party."

Greg roused from his thoughts and realized that dusk had finally settled. He looked at his watch: 10:30! Northern latitudes really lengthened a day.

As Greg climbed the path to the bunkhouse a shaft of light from the open door filtered through the darkened trees.

"Give us a hand with the new guy's canoe, Greg," called a voice.

They stashed the boat in the bushes and carried the paddles into the bright lights and laughter of the party which was getting underway.

"Meet the new man. This here's Mel. It looks like he does his hiking by canoe," said Hank, the self-appointed master of ceremonies, raising his beer can in welcome.

"It's good to be back fellas," said Mel, acknowledging their hospitality. "When I worked in Swan Hills five years back, my buddies and I used to paddle old Beulah down to The Crossroad all the time. You ought to try it."

As conversation wound down, Mel spoke up once more: "I meant it fellas. If any of you want to take my canoe out on the river, just leave a note on my bed and get the blades out of the closet. It's fine with me."

The next day Greg took his fishing rod down to the river to practice casting with some new flies.

"How ya doin' Greg?" said Mel as he came down the path. "On a nice night like this you should have tried out the canoe. I meant what I said about using it if you want to."

Greg enjoyed canoeing, so they talked about making a trip down the the Freeman River.

"You'll need two cars and about three hours for the run, so give yourself plenty of time to be out before the sun goes down."

"If it's nice we could try it tomorrow," Greg suggested.

"Go ahead, but find someone else. I'm busy."

Later that night Greg checked with another summer student, a wiry redhead named Johnny.

"Yeah we can do it tomorrow as long as you know where

you're going because I sure don't," laughed Johnny.

They agreed to meet when they finished work at 4:00.

"Cookie, we'll be back at 5:00. Any chance of an early supper for Johnny and me? It doesn't have to be hot, just something fast."

"Sure thing Greg. If it's not enough, I'll leave you something for later."

Greg and Johnny changed into jeans and T-shirts and drove tandem down to well site 16. They headed through the bush, following the ruts that led to the gravel shingle stretching out into the river known locally as The Crossroad. They dropped off one car and returned to camp, ate and hurried down to the river with the canoe on their shoulders; quite pleased with getting away before 5:30.

"You paddle the stern Greg: I don't know much about a canoe," said Johnny as he climbed in and crept forward. Greg rolled his pants, put his runners and socks in the canoe, and waded into the water, to free the canoe from shore. The sun warmed Greg's back as they slipped along easily with the current.

"Do you see – in that little bay," Johnny asked, pointing with his paddle. "There goes a mallard duck finning along with her brood."

"Look how clear the water is. You can see the rocks on the bottom with minnows darting in and out of the reeds. It's almost as if you could reach out and touch them," Greg observed, resting his paddle for a moment to keep the water still.

Just then Johnny's paddle scraped the bottom. He watched carefully as Greg steered the canoe around the rocks, but soon the water depth was too shallow for safety.

"This is hopeless Johnny. We're going to ruin the bottom of the canoe if we keep this up. I guess the river is lower than Mel figured. With just getting back here, he wouldn't realize how little it's rained. Maybe if we get out and walk, we can float the canoe along until it gets past these rapids."

Greg rolled his jeans higher and stepped into the icy water. Johnny managed to keep his balance even though his runner slipped on the wet moss covered rocks.

"Ouch! This is murder on my bare feet," Greg complained. "Hold on a minute. I have to put my shoes back on."

"Got a match Greg? Mine just fell into the water."

"Nope. I don't smoke."

Slowly they worked their way downstream, pushing the canoe along between them until they passed the rapids and came to deeper water. With sodden shoes, they climbed back into the canoe and continued downstream enjoying the profusion of nature. The sun remained high in the evening sky, spilling its warm yellow light along the banks of the river.

"Look at those would you!" Johnny said as they came upon some peculiar stick mounds extending into the river.

"They're beaver lodges. If we round this next bend very quietly, we might see a beaver working on his dam."

"Are you trying to tell me we found deep water because we're going to come up against a beaver dam downstream?" asked Johnny.

"Yes, but it won't be hard to get the canoe past it. We'll beach the canoe and carry it around on the shore."

They dipped their blades with the stealth of an Indian war party and glided around the next bend in the river to see if they could sneak up on any unsuspecting beaver.

"Hi there!" came a voice from a small punt with two fishermen. "Great day for fishing."

The boys were so surprised to find other people in such an out-of-the-way place, they were speechless for a moment and it showed on their faces.

"You've come across our favorite fishin' hole," said one of the men amiably. "We come here all the time with our bush buggy from The Crossroad and camp just over there," he added, pointing out a battered vehicle parked by an orange two-man tent on the far shore. The men had been there two days and were about to drive back to Fort Assiniboine. Greg and Johnny said their goodbyes and headed downstream.

"Hey fellas," Johnny called back to the men, "Have you got any matches?"

They gave Johnny a light and waved away his extended hand returning the penny matchbook, "Keep'em. You'll want another smoke before you're finished."

"Hey, that's great. Thanks!" and the boys continued their journey down the river.

With all of their talking there wasn't a beaver to be seen, but their destruction was overwhelming. The dammed river overflowed its banks and spilled into little lagoons, turning the low lying ground into swamp. Bushes and trees, trapped in the water were dying and everywhere were the gnawed stumps of young trees.

"There's the beaver dam just ahead," Greg said. "Can you see a low spot where there's a spillway? Maybe we can slip right over."

The dam was a big one. They moved toward the shore, but the shore was non-existent, as high water spilled into the forest. In disgust they climbed out of the canoe, on the top of the dam and worked it over the watery sticks and mud. Downstream the river slowed to a trickle. They pushed on as before, floating the canoe in ankle deep water, and sloshing over the rock strewn river bed. Greg's jeans wouldn't stay rolled and bit-by-bit became wet like Johnny's.

In some places they had to carry the canoe on their shoulders, hooding their vision. Trying to keep it balanced as they constantly slipped on wet rocks and moss was exhausting. The fading sun slipped in the evening sky as they plodded along in silence.

"I was just thinking Johnny. We're taking a chance walking along here this time of night. My mom trains Scout leaders and she says you have to keep talking. If you startle a bear by walking in silence, you may cross between her and her cub and she'll attack. If you make lots of noise as you walk, she'll hear you, find a hiding place and watch you go by. My kid brother has a little bell attached to his backpack."

Greg could sense his own apprehension was making a long story of it, just to keep talking. Now and then they came to parts of the river deep enough to continue paddling. Each time they hoped the water would last, and sometimes it did for several bends.

"Darn! Time to walk again. I didn't expect all these rocks," Greg complained.

On they trudged, their runners aspirating noisily as the water sucked in and out with each step.

"It's 8:30. Our three hours are up. How much farther do you think it will be to The Crossroad?" asked Johnny trying to mask a touch of anxiety in his voice.

"I dunno," Greg answered cautiously. "The river has caused us to lose some time but we haven't stopped. I'd say maybe by nine, nine-thirty, we should make it."

An eerie cry split the air.

"My God! What was that?" shrieked Johnny.

"Don't worry! That's a good sign. It's a loon. If there's a loon around here there must be deep water."

Just then Johnny stumbled. He rolled over, sitting in four inches of water and slapped its surface in a silent oath.

"As if I weren't wet enough!" he fumed as he regained his footing and took hold of his end of the canoe. "Just listen to those dumb birds, sitting there squawking. I think they're laughing at me!"

The commotion had caught the eye of some curious grey jays. Three of them had come to watch the boys and were perched on a nearby branch. Like kids in the booster bleachers at a baseball game, they cheered the boys with raucous enthusiasm.

"Aw, you can't be mad at those birds," Greg teased, trying to get back into a happier frame of mind. "That's the famous Canada Jay. The locals call them whiskeyjacks. They just like to be sociable."

As predicted, they found deeper water and were able to climb back into the boat.

"Where's that loon? I'd like to thank him personally for his private water supply," quipped Johnny.

"Over there, see? There are two of them silhouetted against the setting sun."

"Just what we need, a setting sun," muttered Johnny.

Greg and Johnny rounded one bend after another, each

time expecting to see The Crossroad and each time finding more raw nature. The growth along the river bank seemed drained of color as the lingering sun lost its intensity, and the air became cooler.

H'mm, 9:45. The Crossroad must be nearby, Greg thought. Johnny's paddling quite well for a beginner; strong and rhythmic. The unending crescendo of crickets and frogs dulled their senses. Dip swing, dip swing, dip swing.

"Now hear this. Now hear this," Greg's paddle seemed to say to him.

What a ridiculous thing for me to hear from a paddle, he thought. His mind wandered back to when his mother used the old wringer washing machine at the lake and they would play games listening to its motor, hearing words from its constant groanings.

His wet pants and shoes felt like ice packs on his legs and feet. The strength of the wilderness pressed in from every side. He conceded that he was getting tired, but Johnny was plugging on, so he kept up his rhythm and they slipped along in silence.

"Now hear this. Now hear this ... ," Greg's paddle whispered again. His mind shifted back to his mother. She had her ways, and sometimes, to pry any of her four boys from the television, she would plant herself in front of the TV screen and mimic a ship's captain, saying, "Now hear this. Now here this. This is your mother speaking." Then she would add her important message: "cut the lawn, . . . shovel the snow, . . . or who's finished their homework?" This was the first summer he hadn't had to cut the lawn, Greg mused as he pulled again on his paddle.

"Now hear this. Now hear this," sang Greg's paddle.

Will that crazy thought not leave my head! The last time mom did that was during the winter, he remembered. What was it she wanted? Oh yes, she was waving a piece of paper at us, saying something about it being the next camping lecture for Scout Training and we were to read it because it was something we should know, even if we weren't Scouts. Then she stood there blocking the TV screen until we had all dutifully read it.

"S.T.O.P." is all he could remember from the paper, but his mind kept nagging him. Oh yes, "What to do in an emergency. S for stop, T for think, O for organize and P for plan," or was it "proceed"? The other side of the page was all about hypothermia. His mother's final words sounded in his brain!

"You have to learn about it before it happens! You have to know the circumstances when hypothermia will happen, because once you have the symptoms, your mind won't function well-enough to do anything about it!"

Adrenalin shot through Greg's body. Maybe that's why Johnny is so silent. He just keeps paddling like a mechanical robot. He is a lot wetter than me.

"Hey Johnny," Greg spoke into the silence. There was no answer. "*Hey Johnny*," he shouted.

"Hey Johnny, Hey Johnny, Hey Joh . . ." echoed in the dark sullen hills around them, until all was quiet again.

"What?" Johnny mumbled.

"What d'ya say? You cold? Tired? How's it going?"

No answer. Johnny just kept digging with his paddle.

"Darn, I wish I had read that paper better!" Greg brooded.

"S.T.O.P. – Stop for Emergencies," it had read.

I have to make a decision, thought Greg. Even if The Crossroad and my car are just around the bend, we can't take a chance on bumbling down the river in the dark. Hypothermia, Mom had called it. She said "Do something to prevent it, before it gets you." God, if only I could remember! We are tired and hungry, and worst of all we're cold and wet; perfect candidates! Johnny might already be in trouble.

The sky still seemed light, but the river bank looked darker than ever. It was 10:00 p.m., half an hour until dark. Greg steered for shore and crunched the bow onto the gravel beach. Johnny did not move. Greg heard his voice commanding Johnny to get out: "Pick up the canoe! Good! Now go straight ahead to those bushes." Johnny stood there like a zombie staring into the dark undergrowth.

Greg could see that there was an overhanging mud bank behind the first row of willows. He decided it might be more out of the wind if they camped between the mud bank and the willows where there was a little rise in the beach. He caught Johnny's elbow and urged him forward to the clearing.

Heat! Gotta have heat, his mind ordered. "Come on Johnny, help me get some wood."

There was plenty of dead wood in the bush, but feeling for it in the dark and ripping it free was hard. Johnny didn't help. Greg gathered as big a pile as he could, while Johnny plunked himself down near the woodpile and shivered as he stared at the ground.

Greg was no Boy Scout, but family outings had taught him a few things and soon he had a little pile of birch twigs packed around a wad of spruce resin. Greg searched for the matches; he was getting cold now that it was dark.

"Thank God Johnny got those matches," Greg muttered as he lit the first match.

Zztt. The match scratched across the folder and went out. So did the next one.

Guess I'd better get closer, Greg said to himself. He positioned himself on the windward side of the fire and shielded the operation with his shivering backside to the wind.

Zztt. The match flickered. As he lowered his shaking hands to the branches the flame snuffed out again.

"Cheap matches," Greg growled through jaws clenched with muscle spasms. Carefully he clutched the flimsy package in the darkness and tore away a fourth match. It was all he could do to strike the match as his fingers willfully jerked and floundered in the night air.

Try again. Easy does it. You've only got two left, penetrated his thoughts. Plant your elbows and keep those hands still! Do it right for God's sake!

He struck the next match: Zztt. The little flame held and he lowered it the one inch to his lump of resin. Slowly the tension in his body released as the flame spread to the twigs. He fed the spot of light carefully, placing bigger branches near the flames until he was sure the night winds could not rob him of success.

The heat felt good and Greg got Johnny to come close to

the fire. It was now 11:00 p.m. and pitch black except for the flickering ring of light on the mud bank and the glow of their tired faces in the firelight.

"Jeez my rear end's cold. This is supposed to be summer?!" Greg swore to the world in general. He took off his wet shoes and pushed his feet into the clammy sand, then raised them near the flames. The heat felt good. Now for the waiting, he thought.

"Hey Johnny, have you ever stayed in the bush all night? Johnny, are you listening to me?"

Johnny just shivered and stared at the fire. Greg's adrenalin rose again as he realized Johnny really was in trouble.

Gotta do something, but what?

"He's cold, but how do I get him warm?" The voice Greg heard was his own but it seemed to be a comfort.

"Come on Johnny, off with that wet T-shirt," Greg said quickly putting his own dry shirt on Johnny. Next came Johnny's shoes, socks, pants and undershorts. The body of Greg's pants were dry and would just have to do him while Johnny wore Greg's T-shirt, underwear and the socks he had kept dry in the canoe. Greg sat Johnny by the fire and dropped the wet clothes over a bush near the fire. He smoothed Johnny's wet socks onto the hot rocks around the fire and peeled their runners open as he set them in the heat to dry. Next he dragged the canoe up behind them and propped it with rocks to cut the wind from the river and trap the heat from the fire between its concave interior and the mud bank.

The thought of going into the bush again in total darkness, groping his way to search for more wood was insane, but he could see no other way as the fire burned ravenously and was depleting the wood pile. Submissively, Greg tugged on his damp runners and plunged into the forest; his arms up to protect his head and chest from the wanton branches. Feeling his way in the dark, he found dead wood much farther than he had gone before. Each time the light of the fire was there to guide him back. Greg slaved on until he collapsed with exhaustion.

The inactivity was chilling.

"1:30. What a lousy way to spend a night!"

Greg built a bigger fire and rested. The silence was broken only by the crackle of the flames, and the furtive rustling of leaves as if some animal were in retreat. Johnny felt warm against Greg's bare top as he snuggled down beside his sleeping friend to share his body heat.

Time slipped by as Greg gazed into the fire and watched the flames sink lower and lower as if they were part of a ritual dance that would come to an end. Lord, I've never been so cold, he thought.

Cold! With this he came to his senses. "The fire! Can't let it go out!" Greg screamed into the darkness and dragged himself over to the woodpile, fully awake again.

"Won't this night ever end?" he cried.

With the fire renewed, Greg checked the clothes bush. Johnny's T-shirt and socks were dry so he put them on. "Hmm, not my color scheme, but warm." At least he had his sense of humor. He felt Johnny's jeans and replaced them near the heat.

"Come on Johnny, don't go to sleep on me. Help me keep the fire going or we'll freeze."

Greg couldn't make any sense of Johnny's mumbled reply. The shoes were dry. Greg put his own runners on again and struggled to get Johnny's feet into his shoes. The warm rock the shoes had been sitting on felt good and Greg cradled it in his hands.

"Hey Johnny, wake up! Here, hold this rock in your lap, maybe it'll make you feel better."

The flames leapt higher and Johnny stirred.

"Wha' gives?" he blurted. "Wha's goin' on?"

"Don't you remember?" Greg asked.

Looking around, Johnny ruffled his hair. "I'm cold. Where's m' pants?"

"Drying," Greg answered. The pants were dry so he tugged them onto his helpless friend.

Johnny was dozing again. Greg shook him gently, saying: "Why don't you have a cigarette?"

Greg lit one in the fire and put it between Johnny's fingers. Johnny roused and had a puff.

"Wha' time is it? It's so dark." he mumbled.

"Don't ask. There are ninety minutes in every hour. Lucky for us your cigarettes and matches stayed dry when you fell in. I was sure glad to have those matches."

Johnny wasn't listening and the cigarette threatened to burn his fingers. Greg realized it was hard to keep him awake. Johnny needed help! For the next hour Greg kept the fire blazing and prodded and talked to Johnny as they cradled warm rocks and huddled together in the curved backdrop of the canoe.

"Will this night never end?!" Greg moaned when he noticed the woodpile growing low again.

Greg watched the black and greys of the forest finally take on color at 5:00 a.m. The river was shrouded in mist and upwind Greg could see the dim outline of a deer drinking at the water's edge. The rays of sunlight shone through the mist and warmed his shoulders as he kicked sand over the fire. Greg dragged himself and the canoe back to the shore, then helped his friend down to the river.

"Wha' happened to our canoe trip?" Johnny wanted to know.

The current was strong, Greg couldn't believe it was the same river that had confounded them the night before. The mist lifted and the river glistened in all its morning splendor as the current carried them along the first few bends. It was 5.45.

"Halloo," Mel bellowed as they came around a bend in the river. "Greg! Johnny! Over here, on the bank!" he called motioning them to cut toward the shore. "Boy, am I glad to see you two guys," he grinned as he caught the front of the canoe.

"You're a beautiful sight yourself!" Greg sighed.

"Let me paddle there Johnny," Mel said, noticing Johnny more closely and the idle paddle in the center of the canoe. "We'll pick up the cars and I'll radio the company to call off the search party they were getting together for this morning. Then we'll get back to camp and feed you guys," Mel added to encourage them as he set his big shoulders to work.

They paddled toward The Crossroad, content to let Mel carry on with his friendly monologue.

"I got your note that you had the boat Greg. When I realized you were overdue, I notified the company and came out last night to look for you. As soon as I saw the river I realized it was too low and knew what had happened. I camped by the cars overnight, and put a light on shore so you couldn't pass by in the dark. I hiked out here this morning to see if I could find you. I just hoped there was enough camper in the two of you to survive hypothermia. Older hands than you two have bought it out here in the bush y'know. You don't get a second chance!"

Greg checked his watch: 7:10. Had they tried to keep going last night it would have been close to one a.m. before they reached The Crossroad. Two or more hours in the dark; cold, wet and totally exhausted. Mel was right, but they *had* survived. Greg wasn't sure what they had done right but he was determined that before it happened again, he would find out!

Part B
What You Should Know About Hypothermia

Ignorance on the part of helpers and rescuers has often led to dangerously incorrect treatment being given to those suffering from exposure.

British Mountaineering Council
(circular #380)

Hypothermia, brought on by chilling the inner core of the body, is a unique illness that makes you mentally incapable of good judgement quite early in its onset. To protect yourself from becoming a victim of hypothermia you must be able to recognize the body's early reactions to cold, warning you to rest and warm yourself. You must also be able to recognize the environmental conditions that promote this emergency so you can seek cover in time to protect yourself.

To protect your companions, you must be knowledgeable about the symptoms of mild and profound hypothermia, and how to treat them, for once they are under its influence, they will not be able to treat themselves.

Even with good planning, you might still find yourself exposed to the illness, so it is important to be sure your companions are also knowledgeable about the illness and capable of coming to your assistance! You must all know about the prevention, recognition and treatment of hypothermia, as a team effort, as it is the most effective.

2

Prevention
of Hypothermia

Those with experience in the wilderness take the possibility of hypothermia very seriously in *all* seasons. With good planning and organization they attempt to prevent it as their first line of defense against succumbing to this silent killer. Factors in preventing hypothermia include understanding the illness, undertaking the necessary planning before going into the wilderness, and maintaining and conserving energy along the trail.

Understanding Hypothermia

To understand hypothermia, you must understand the internal and external forces which affect body heat and how body heat is produced or lost. This information is presented under the following headings:

- The Physiology of the Human Body
- The Physics of Body Heat Loss
- The Weather Conditions that Lead to Hypothermia

The Physiology of Body Heat Loss

For prevention and treatment of hypothermia it is important to have an understanding of the physiology of the human body regarding those functions involved in defending itself against cold. This knowledge is the *basis* for being able to make quick, accurate decisions when faced with the difficult circumstances of this illness. There are five aspects of human physiology related to the body's defense against cold.

Man's Origin and Evolution

Man originated in tropical climates of 28 °C (82 °F). Over the years, Man has been able to migrate to cooler climates by using technology for improved insulation against cold and a suitable diet. Now, within the civilized areas of temperate and cold climates, we tend to take the improvements afforded in the design of clothing, heated dwellings, transportation and communication, for granted.

Despite migration during evolution, Man's physiological reaction to cold has not changed. Even today, Man can withstand hunger and thirst far longer than he can withstand cold. Man must provide for his own defense against the cold if he ventures into uncivilized areas, to ensure that his body will continue to function properly. He must provide for a proper diet, insulated clothing, shelter and the ability to make heat.

The Significance of Man Being Warm-Blooded

As with warm-blooded animals, the human body gains energy from food and expends energy creating body heat and activity, both physical and mental. Activity and metabolism of food regularly make far more heat than is necessary to keep the body warm. Normally the body loses large amounts of excess heat; which is of no consequence until it is faced with cold conditions. When cold sensors within the body are activated by chilling, the body initiates special functions to prevent heat loss and increase the production of heat.

The human body, using energy, is primarily heated from within by chemical reactions controlled by the brain, not by the sun or applied heat. This means that the body's own mechanisms can produce warmth in its inner core more effectively than a first aider can by physically warming the outside surfaces of the victim's body. In treating hypothermia, it is more effective to work *with body physiology* rather than against it. Your prime ways to assist the body in maintaining heat are:

a) energy conservation by rest, and
b) insulating the victim against further heat loss.

Man's Physiological Reaction to Cold

The human body is designed to function within about 1 °C of 37 °C (taken orally). Below this normal temperature range, various life support systems start to fail. For example, as body temperature decreases:

– enzyme and chemical reactions become increasingly slower and finally fail at a temperature unique to each individual type of enzyme or chemical reaction.
– body fluids such as blood, increase in viscosity, inhibiting proper circulation.

The original health of the person and the amount of chilling that their life support systems can withstand varies with each individual, however as the chilling progresses, within all individuals, the rate of body malfunction progressively increases.

When threatened with cold, the two nervous systems of the body receive messages from their cold sensors to initiate special functions in an effort to maintain normal body temperature.

The Somatic Nervous System receives thought patterns that give you specific messages in your conscious brain to prevent heat loss. These specific messages might be: put on more clothes, turn up the heat, get out of the draft, rest under a warm blanket, sit in the sun, etc. You appear to just happen to think of something you should do to make yourself warmer by preventing heat loss, and you consciously carry out those directions to prevent getting colder.

The Autonomic Nervous System automatically carries messages to all parts of the body, without your conscious knowledge, initiating special functions that produce and conserve heat in an effort to prevent the body from cooling below 37°C. Two less complex functions that you can easily recognize are shivering and getting goose bumps; neither of which you can summon or control with your conscious brain. Shivering is a form of muscular work to create heat and goose bumps are formed to hold the hair follicle upright to increase the insulating quality of the hairs in protecting the skin from the cold.

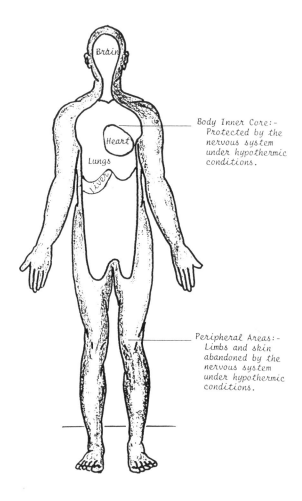

Body Inner Core:-
Protected by the
nervous system
under hypothermic
conditions.

Peripheral Areas:-
Limbs and skin
abandoned by the
nervous system
under hypothermic
conditions.

The Body's Inner Core and Peripheral Areas

The Autonomic Nervous System requires huge amounts of energy to initiate these protective life sustaining physiological changes despite the body's other needs for energy to supply heat and activity.

All complex functions initiated by the two nervous systems to combat prolonged chilling of the body strive to maintain 37°C in the main organs essential to life. When exposed to prolonged chilling, the body will abandon peripheral areas of limbs and skin, allowing them to lower in temperature, before it allows the essential organs of the inner core of the body to follow with a lower temperature.

The brain, lungs, heart, liver, hormone and endocrine systems among other organs, all located in the body inner core, cooperate in this very complex physiological change that attempts to protect the stability of the inner core temperature, to ensure the continued function of these life sustaining organs.

Energy Waste and Total Energy Supply

Unfortunately, most of the protective changes the body initiates, produce side effects that in themselves waste energy, which depletes the body's limited supply of energy, in ever increasing amounts. Three examples of this are:

a) *Activity of Large Muscles to Produce Heat.* This would appear to be a beneficial action as activity can produce body heat faster than the heat produced by metabolism. However, activity requires energy for the work accomplished as well as energy for the heat produced in doing that work, whether it is useful work such as chopping wood, useless work such as walking back and forth to stay warm, or subconscious work such as shivering. Although the heat produced sustains the body, that rise in body temperature increases the temperature difference between the body and its environment. The bigger the temperature difference, the more heat lost from the body to the air, necessitating more work to stay warm.

b) *By Intake Of Food.* More nutrients should increase body energy. However before this new supply of energy can be available to the body, energy is required to digest that food, at a time when there is no energy to spare for digestion, without endangering some other important function. Digestion will be slow and difficult. In actual fact, tests show that eating will first cause a drop in inner core temperature, the opposite result from what was wanted.

c) *Additional Metabolism for More Heat Production.* When activated by cold sensors, the body automatically increases metabolism for more heat. However, metabolism requires oxygen. In breathing more oxygen to sustain higher metabolism (seen by you as puffing) to produce body heat, you take vast quantities of air into your lungs, heat it, moisture it, use the oxygen out of the air and breathe the remainder of the warmed air out. This represents tremendous heat loss. Metabolism may produce heat, but the required breathing causes more heat loss; an endless circle of need and loss.

In these three examples, when the body increased heat production through activity, ingesting more nutrients, or increasing metabolism, there was always heat wasted in the process, causing an ever increasing need and loss of energy.

This understanding of human physiology, should also lead you to recognize that you can minimize heat loss on the trail by following these three rules.

1. Don't allow yourself to get overheated. Always remove some of your layered clothing to maintain comfort when you are active.

2. When cold and tired on the trail, have a sweet drink but don't indulge in heavy eating as it will deplete your energy needed for warmth.

3. When threatened with cold, conserve energy by working at a reduced pace so that you get the job done but not at the risk of labored breathing.

The management of your total body energy supply is the essence of survival in a hypothermic situation. The body sustains life by using energy to carry out functions required by it. The body has instant energy available for use and stored energy. Under normal circumstances, the instantly available energy is sufficient to carry out all of the body's necessary functions. With prolonged chilling, vast quantities of energy are required for normal function, for additional heat and activity against the cold, for initiating complex physiological changes to protect the body inner core temperature and for the waste of energy encountered in the production of heat. The body's supply of instantly available energy is limited, at the onset of the chilling process, to that energy gained from the last meal and snacks, plus a little of your stored energy. The liver's function to transpose stored energy (glycogen) to useful energy (glucose) is too slow to produce the enormous supply of energy necessary to combat hypothermia. You can recognize that a person cannot lose twenty pounds in an hour just because the body needs that energy. Prolonged chilling kills because the body runs out of instantly available energy, despite its complex system to conserve and preserve the functions of the vital organs. Understanding how the body uses energy and what actions you can undertake to manage energy wisely, may save your life.

The Body's Ability to Accept Outside Help

The body responds well to outside help of insulation, warmth, rest and nourishment when this help is offered with the body temperature still at 37°C. The lower the body temperature drops, the more advanced the hypothermia will be. The more advanced the hypothermia is, the less effective any help will be because of diminished body functions capable of accepting that help.

Conclusion and Recommendation

Body physiology is such that it cannot combat cold on its own for a long period of time; it needs help and that help is much more effective when given early in the chilling process.

The Physics of Body Heat Loss

Preventing heat loss from the body is the most effective way Man has to combat hypothermia in the field. To prevent heat loss, one must understand the four ways in which the body loses heat: radiation, conduction, convection and evaporation.

Radiation is the movement of infrared heat waves away

from the heat source. The bigger the difference in temperature between the heat source and the environment, the greater the heat loss. That is, the colder the weather, the warmer the person or the smaller the person, by weight, the greater percentage of heat loss from the body.

Conduction occurs when two objects are in physical contact, and heat passes from the molecules of the warmer object to those of the cooler object. The rate of heat transfer increases, the larger the area of contact and the greater the difference in temperature of the two objects. In the field, that heat lost by conduction will depend on the size of the area in contact: whether you are standing, sitting or laying down, and the insulating quality of the surfaces in contact.

Conduction is also important within the body. Inner layers of tissue are cooled by contact with cold outer layers of tissue. Under normal conditions all tissue is warmed by heat transfer as warm blood circulates through the body. Under hypothermic conditions the body protects the inner core from wasting heat on peripheral areas, or being chilled by blood returning from these areas, by restricting the blood supply to peripheral areas. This in turn, limits the harmful conduction of heat. If your hands and feet are cold while hiking, your body is trying to protect you from mild hypothermia.

Convection is similar to conduction, but with one of the temperature areas in motion. One form of convection is *air or water moving* around Man. Various forces continually move air or water warmed by the body, away from it, thus perpetuating the minimum air or water temperature in contact with the higher temperature of Man, which causes maximum heat loss from Man's body. Air convection combined with cold is measured as the windchill factor. To combat heat loss by air convection in the field, you must get out of the wind.

A second form of convection can be caused by *Man moving* and causing air or water to rush past him to produce the maximum loss of body heat. Sailing, jogging, cycling, scuba diving, swimming and skiing are all examples of Man in motion producing cooling by convection. To reduce heat loss, Man must slow down or stop his activity.

Evaporation occurs when water boils, vaporizes or freezes, depending on the available heat it can absorb from its surroundings. Man's skin has a natural moisture and can also be wet from perspiration or environmental causes. Under the conditions presented by the body heat at 37°C, moisture on the skin will always vaporize, by absorbing body heat, as dictated by the laws of physics. Vaporization demands huge quantities of heat from the body, representing a tremendous drain of body energy. The best protection from heat loss by evaporation is to stay dry.

Four Ways in which the Body Loses Heat

1. *Radiation*: Heat radiates from the body through clothing and from exposed skin. The body gains some heat by radiation from the sun.

2. *Conduction*: Heat is conducted away from the body where it touches the ground or other objects such as this log.

3. *Convection*: Maximum loss of heat is experienced from air or water moving against the body.

4. *Evaporation*: Heat from the body is used to evaporate moisture of perspiration, the mucous membranes of the mouth and nose, and environmental dampness.

Conclusion and Recommendation

Of radiation, conduction, convection and evaporation; convection and evaporation are the most important for Man to control in the prevention of heat loss. In combating hypothermia, you must stay dry and out of the wind to minimize the effects of convection and evaporation.

Weather Conditions for Hypothermia

Weather can change rapidly. You must be prepared for bad weather as well as the forecast which was predicted by the weather bureau. A drop in barometric pressure signals deteriorating weather and may produce a combination of wind, cold and moisture that will maximize body heat loss. Although bad weather is often perceived as a singular problem, you must understand the threat posed by each of the three elements individually.

Wind

Whether it is a strong wind or a light breeze, wind cools by convection. Exposed skin loses heat much faster than clothed skin. In moderate temperatures, bare arms and legs may feel great, but you have no way of knowing how much extra heat and energy, which you may need later, is being lost. Wind pushes cold air through your hair and clothes, driving heat away from you. Therefore, wear a hat, stay properly zipped up, belted down or tucked in, with just enough layers of clothing to be comfortable without perspiring.

Cold

Hypothermia happens most often in temperatures above freezing, 0°C to 10°C (32°F to 50°F). It happens at these relatively warm temperatures more than at below freezing because people, thinking these temperatures are not dangerous, don't take precautions to conserve energy along the trail or stay absolutely dry. For example: moderate cold vaporizes moisture, something you cannot see happening. This allows you to ignore heat loss by evaporation. Extreme cold freezes moisture and you can see your breath and frost on your hair and you take more care.

Moisture

Even with the best rain (snow) gear, or the greatest precaution, it is difficult to stay dry when hiking. The moisture you experience may be rain, drizzle, mist, dew, snow or surface water that splashes on your clothes. You may wear unventilated rain gear or too many clothes and perspire. No matter what the cause of the moisture, evaporation will demand heat for vaporization and this heat loss is one of the oldest forms of refrigeration known to man. It effectively lowers the temperature of your clothing below the environmental temperature.

Have you ever stood outside wearing a a wet bathing suit and towel? Then you know that you feel cold from evaporation until the sun "dries" you, no matter how warm the day is. This is because the water evaporating from your wet suit and towel is drawing heat from your body as well as from the sun, to dry your clothes. You feel cold because the heat demanded for evaporation has made the skin next to your wet bathing suit colder than the environmental temperature.

Water conducts heat away from the body 25 to 30 times faster than air. This means that if your clothes are damp you will lose heat 25 to 30 times faster than if they were dry and subjected to the same temperature conditions. With wind added to your problems, the cooling will be even faster.

The water temperature at most indoor public swimming pools is kept about 25°C. With moderate activity, most swimmers have enough energy to enjoy a public pool for about one hour. By that time they feel tired and cold, figure they have had enough and head for the warm showers or hot pool. Can you imagine the energy reserve necessary to keep you warm in 10°C water? That is the temperature your perspiration damp or rain-wet clothing will be if the environmental temperature is 10°C; less if you take the refrigeration effect of evaporation into account. By deduction this means that your energy will be stressed in less than an hour if you are wearing wet or damp clothing at 10°C; a fairly acceptable hiking temperature.

Conclusions and Recommendations

Wet or perspiration damp clothing spell *danger*: you will chill 25 to 30 times faster. Change damp clothing immediately.

Do not underestimate moderate cold: it will drain your energy if there is insufficient insulation in your clothing. Being wet at 10° C can be fatal.

Be wary of wind, work at staying dry, and carry an extra jacket or sweater for times of rest or a lower environmental temperature.

It is usually the combination of wind, moisture and cold that kills!

Recognizing the Symptoms of Hypothermia

The normal oral body temperature is 37°C (98.6°F). Use of a thermometer is an exact way to determine the degree of hypothermia being suffered by a victim, however, the average clinical thermometer has a low range of 34°C and is not suitable for determining hypothermia. The use of a low reading thermometer in the field is difficult and most experienced outdoor persons tend to rely on visual symptoms of the victim in making their decisions.

The physiology of every victim differs, making it impossible to apply exact temperatures at which different symptoms will manifest themselves. There are, however, three distinct stages between the onset of cooling in the body inner core and death.

Early Warning Signs of Hypothermia: 37°C Cooling to 36°C

Early warning signs of hypothermia will be recognized in yourself more quickly than under observation from others. However, as more outdoors experience is gained the more these signs become obvious in yourself and in the group.

You may feel cool and somewhat tired, especially during rest stops and you will receive the thought message to recognize you are cold. Your body metabolism will increase to cause warmth, seen by you as heavier breathing and an increased pulse rate. Subconsciously you will be inclined to stamp your feet, rub your hands, keep walking down the trail in dogged determination to reach your goal (the campsite, your car, etc.) or you won't want to stop and rest when the others do.

All of these subconscious activities are the autonomic nervous system compelling the muscles to do work to keep the body warm, something you can recognize if you understand the process. Your body will make heat, by work expressed as tension: with goose bumps, holding arms tightly wrapped around the body for added insulation or hunching of shoulders to protect from cooling around the neck. Finally you may start to shiver on and off as your metabolism maintains warmth at times and doesn't need to maintain warmth at other times, depending on your activity and wind shifts. By shivering, your body is making additional work for warmth because your useful work, say walking, is not sufficient to maintain heat and the body is getting desperate.

These symptoms don't sound so bad. In an emergency you might even think you can ignore these signs, relying on your strength and endurance to carry you through. However, you must recognize these warning signs and immediately take precautions against further heat loss to avoid becoming a victim of mild hypothermia.

Symptoms of Mild Hypothermia: 36°C cooling to 32°C

36°C to 35°C - You are moving toward a state where you may not attempt to save yourself and must rely on your companions and a cooperative group effort for effective relief from the cold. With mild hypothermia you often have trouble keeping up with the group's pace and will likely begin to show negative opinions. You will complain of being cold and getting warm will become your main objective. Physical symptoms include increased shivering especially when inactive, fumbling hands and numbness of skin. You and your companions will now recognize you have a hypothermic problem. The sooner you move to prevent heat loss, the longer you will maintain your dwindling energy reserves.

35 °C *to* 34 °C - By this time you will be unable to perform in a responsible fashion to save yourself. You will have to rely on help from your companions. You become obsessed with trying to stay warm at any cost and begin intense shivering, mental and physical activity is slow and labored, you have difficulty with slurred speech, incompetent hands, lurching gait, the tendency to stumble on uneven ground, a frequent urge to urinate, mild confusion and inattentiveness to those around you.

34 °C *to* 32 °C - At this point you are totally at the mercy of the environment, and are unable to think or act in a rational manner. You are unable to use your hands and may not let your friends help you. You begin violent shivering, and you will have periods of amnesia, depression, difficulty with speaking and difficulty using your large muscle groups (those which facilitate standing or sitting).

Symptoms of Profound Hypothermia: 32°C and Lower

The medical profession divides this stage into moderate hypothermia, 32 °C cooling down to 28 °C, and severe hypothermia, below 28 °C. For the outdoor person these two stages can be considered together, as profound hypothermia.

As the victim's inner core temperature nears and drops below 32 °C several distinct new symptoms manifest themselves. At 32 °C the muscle spasms and shivering cease as the body runs out of energy for this activity. The mental attitude of the victim changes from doing everything possible to keep warm, to complete disregard for keeping mitts or hat on, coat zipped, the extra protection of blankets in place, etc. They may start to disrobe, scattering equipment and clothing necessary to survival along the route. The victim's mental processes will be very slow, showing difficulty in making decisions and in remembering facts such as names or dates. The victim's decisions will exhibit poor judgement with little or no regard for self-protection. The victim may also have a fruity acetone smell to his or her breath and urine soaked clothing.

The victim may have periods of clumsy activity and times when he wants to lay down and sleep. As the body temperature drops, the periods of inactivity will grow longer until the victim cannot be roused. The victim continues to sink towards unconsciousness and rigidity as the body attempts to shut down all functions in an effort to maintain a spark of life in the heart and lungs. The victim needs immediate medical attention. Life may continue until approximately 25°C; although survival has been recorded at much lower temperatures. It is very difficult to distinguish the coma of severe hypothermia from death because there appears to be no pulse or breathing.

You can see that these symptoms are severe! What you *must recognize* is that you can change from showing early warning signs of hypothermia to having mild hypothermia in minutes. Suppose you have been plugging on to your goal, continuing to think you have that extra bit of reserve to see you through. You think, I'm a bit tired and it's getting colder out, but just one more little rest and then I'll go on again and get there. In that rest, without the warmth created by the exercise of walking, you will chill considerably especially if you fail to add an extra jacket for increased insulation while resting, or sitting on the cold ground. That drop in body temperature might be just enough to send you into shivering and begin illogical thinking. If alone, you won't have the mental power to save yourself. You will likely choose to plug on and be completely exhausted. The others may be in as much danger as you are, or you may resist their help by disagreeing with them, determined to continue on, by yourself if need be, with perhaps none of them recognizing that you are under the spell of mild hypothermia.

Conclusion and Recommendation

Any *one* of the symptoms of mild hypothermia or profound hypothermia is cause for alarm. With an oral body temperature below 35.5°C the victim won't think of personal safety and will move toward death unless someone else saves them. You must try to prevent hypothermia before it threatens you. Never ignore shivering!

Planning for Survival Against Hypothermia

In making any plan where you or your companions will be away from easy access to civilization, think ahead, *think hypothermia.*

Personal Factors in Planning for Survival

1. Keep your body in good physical condition with strong muscles, endurance ability and little excess fat.

2. Learn about as many aspects of the wilderness and nature, first aid, weather, physical stress and leadership as you possibly can.

3. Keep up-to-date with the latest technical improvements for survival. Always have equipment close at hand that will aid survival, by dressing sensibly, and carrying things of use in your pockets, backpack and vehicle. (See Appendix B.) Know how to use the equipment effectively and have it in good repair. The most important items to carry for survival refer to protection against water, wind and cold.

4. When you read of accidents, go through the mental exercise of what you would have done in the same circumstances considering your ability and usual equipment. Whenever you don't have a successful answer, plan to improve your knowledge and equipment accordingly. Although not a real experience for you, it will help you to set your frame of mind toward positive reactions. Positive reactions are a necessary ability to avoid panic and maintain control of the situation in a real emergency.

General Factors in Planning for Survival

1. Have a workable plan suitable to your abilities, the area, the weather and one that is possible to complete within the time allowed. Stick to the plan and give a copy of it to a responsible person who is not going with you; someone who will raise the alarm if you don't return on schedule.

2. Know the laws and regulations of the area, such as the need to sign in and out with forestry services; laws regarding

trespassing, firearms, avalanche control and hunting season; hunting season dates; open fire regulations and degree of fire risk for that day, etc.

3.   Know the area and have maps. Know the general topographical features such as which way the mountain ridges or hills run, the direction the river flows, and the location of features such as railways, cutlines, roads, huts, towns or work camps.

4.   Know the weather by having an up-to-date forecast and knowing the usual weather pattern for the area at that time of year.

5.   Know your travelling companions. Know their strengths, weaknesses, abilities, trustworthiness, loyalty and disposition. For safety, have at least four in the group so that you can have two groups of two in the event of an emergency that necessitates splitting the group to go for help.

6.   Know your equipment. Know that it suits your needs for the specific trip you have planned. Take what you need, not too much or too little. Of special importance are protective clothing, protective shelter and fire starter. (See Chapter 5.)

7.   Plan food and drink to suit the outing, plus a little extra. Include water and sweet snacks for along the trail. Eat well before starting out. Choose a menu with high energy and easy digestion. Include proteins, fats and carbohydrates. Have the capability of purifying natural sources of water. (See Chapter 5.)

Conserving and Maintaining Energy along the Trail

Every person has a limit to his or her total energy reserves. These reserves supply the energy for body heat, mental activity and muscular activity. By using energy for activity wisely and protecting yourself against heat loss from the onset of the trip, you may think more clearly and be warmer during an unexpected emergency, and thus escape hypothermia.

Plan Activity Wisely

In everything you do, consider how that activity will affect your consumption of energy. Work and walk in a controlled fashion. Do not indulge in unnecessary horseplay, running, useless activities, walking unnecessary distances or undertaking occupations that overtax your energy. Exchange heavy packs and trade trail breaking and bucking the wind for those most able. In cold weather, make the most of heat from the sun in your choice of trail, rest stops and campsites. In hot weather, make the most of the shade for protection. Plan for rest. Start out with a good night's sleep. Rest after meals for digestion to take place. Stop and relax often along the trail.

Avoid Loss of Body Heat

It is important to continually monitor changes in your environment. Watch the weather for storms, so that you are prepared with your rain gear on, your tent up, or whatever appropriate actions are needed for protection from mist, rain or snow *before* you get wet. Judge every undertaking, even the simple ones such as stopping for a rest, with a determination to stay dry. Change wet clothing. Stay out of the wind by using protective clothing and covering.

Use Food and Drink to Maintain Energy

Start your trip with adequate food supplies to cover the Caloric requirements of the group for the whole trip. Eat well-planned meals and snacks and drink adequate fluids regularly throughout the day. Avoid eating foods that are hard to digest when you are overtired, cold, or on the trail. (See Chapter 5.)

Conclusion and Recommendation

Maintaining an energy reserve throughout the trip is of utmost importance in the event a hypothermic situation develops. Responsible decision making in all aspects of planning and execution of your trip includes how those decisions affect your ability to protect your reserve energy supply.

3

Recognition of
Hypothermia in the Field

Recognition of hypothermia in its early stages can be very difficult. You must be constantly alert to changing conditions of weather, time and human stamina. The better prepared you are when you start out and the earlier hypothermia is recognized as a problem, the better your chances of survival.

Plan to Recognize Hypothermia before You Start Out

1.   Discuss hypothermia within the group. Everyone should be aware of its dangers and the need for defensive planning.

2.   Instruct each member how to test for physical incapacity caused by chilling of the body.

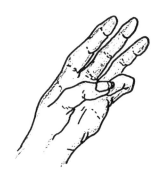

Test for Thermal Incapacity

If you cannot complete this simple maneuver, you must begin some means of warming and resting your body.

With fingers of the same hand, touch your thumb to the tip of your little finger. If you cannot complete this simple maneuver, you are becoming chilled and must begin some means of stopping body heat loss and warm and rest your body. Use this test for thermal incapacity any time you feel cold or tired.

3.   Appoint one member of the group to be the monitor responsible for calling rest periods, keeping track of the time and watching for hypothermia. This person should be the least likely candidate for hypothermia. Base this decision on physical stamina, size, lightest pack, best protected or most rested, or any other appropriate qualities. The monitor is responsible for setting a pace that everyone in the group can maintain, and watching for signs of exhaustion and hypothermia, especially in the smallest and weakest members of the group. The monitor should invite anyone in the group who feels tired, cold or uncomfortable with the pace, to speak up rather than stress themselves.

Criteria for Making the Decision to Stop

1.   If anyone shows signs of mild hypothermia you must stop make camp and treat them.

2.   If darkness falls before there is certainty of relief, stop in sufficient time to make camp during daylight.

3.   If one of your group shows signs of stress, consider that the remaining members of the group will likely show signs of stress in the near future. Stop while there are still some members of the group fit enough to treat the victim and make camp.

4.   If the victim urges you to think he is fit to continue do not take a chance. Stop, rest and be sure that everyone is warm, rested and nourished before continuing.

5.   If you do stop to make camp, remember that in stopping everyone may cool down and become victims. Therefore watch for this among the group and stay sufficiently active to stay warm while treating the victim and making camp.

6.   Do not ignore shivering! Stop before you are exhausted.

Hypothermia may be your initial problem or it may be a secondary emergency compounding situations such as bad weather, getting lost or an accident. If the person watching for signs of exhaustion or hypothermia deems it necessary to stop or if anyone in the group declares themselves a risk you must stop, make camp and begin treatment immediately. Lay short term plans for getting the situation of hypothermia under control, and leave the longer range planning for relief to the first occasion when you can deal with it by group agreement.

In the Event of an Emergency S.T.O.P.

Not all emergencies involve hypothermia. The acronym S.T.O.P. is a memory peg that will help you to make decisions in any emergency. Memorize what it stands for! Often one senses the conditions that will precipitate hypothermia. This premonition is emergency enough to Stop, Think, Organize and Plan. You may prevent it or at least minimize the hypothermia by being prepared in advance through S.T.O.P.

S – *Stop* and gather your group together. Don't panic. Assess what your real problems and dangers are.

T – *Think* of all the things you have: in your pockets, in your food supplies, in your equipment and in your collective brain power. Then think how best to use these things in your situation.

O – *Organize* yourselves and gear to cause the least wear and tear on your bodies and to give the most efficiency. Choose a leader. Your party may have been working under a natural leader by unspoken agreement. At this time, you will be making a choice by majority vote. The decision may elect the natural leader or it may be another, considered more suitable under the circumstances. Take care in choosing your leader; a leader suffering from mild hypothermia will make bad decisions.

P – *Plan* a course of action through group discussion, considering your location, timing, equipment and abilities, with the leader having the deciding vote. When a plan has been completed, delegate the responsibilities and proceed with the plan. From time to time reassess your fatigue, progress and the possibilities of reaching your goal.

Conclusion and Recommendation

Knowledge of hypothermia, combined with good planning, leading to early recognition, minimize the trauma of an hypothermic emergency. Memorize the meaning of the acronym S.T.O.P.

4

Treatment of
Hypothermia in the Field

The circumstances surrounding a hypothermic emergency will vary widely, so no one course of action can be set forth as the only way to manage the situation. The first aider must rely on his knowledge and experience to make sound decisions regarding treatment of this illness.

Not only must the first victim be treated, but the rest of the group must be protected from becoming chilled. Memorize the list of *basic rules* and learn the detailed list of ideas that may help in your situation. This will assist you in making quick, wise decisions regarding your circumstances, the victim, your assistants and available resources.

Theory for Treating Hypothermia in the Field

In treating hypothermia in the field, the first aider is not merely trying to apply heat to the external surfaces of the victim's body. The goal is to prevent further heat loss from the inner core of that person's body, using every means available.

Body Physiology

Apply your knowledge of body physiology and its automatic responses to cooling. The treatment should enhance the body's efforts to maintain inner core warmth, not work against these physiological phenomena. Insulate the body first, then consider means of warming it. When the body core temperature of the victim is *above* 32°C, you can apply heat in any manner you can achieve, striving for those methods you know will be most effective with inner core warmth but nevertheless acting as quickly as possible to produce relief of any kind for the victim. *Below* 32°C, you *must* apply your knowledge of body core physiology. Do not warm peripheral areas; insulate them to provide protection from the cold and premature warming. Apply heat in ways that assist only the inner core to be warmed, to ensure it continues to function until medical assistance has been found.

Be Gentle

Victims of hypothermia must be treated very gently when lifting, moving or undressing them. They must not be asked to perform any activity that will take muscle power as this use of energy will further cool the body's inner core. They should be assisted in activities that cannot be avoided in the course of treatment or rescue. In more advanced cases of hypothermia, 32°C or lower, the vital organs of the body's inner core become very sensitive to rough treatment. With rough treatment the heart may react by losing its rhythm, going very fast or stopping.

Early Treatment

Early treatment is important in preventing "Early Warning Signs of Hypothermia" from degenerating to the more serious symptoms of "Mild Hypothermia" and the critical symptoms of "Profound Hypothermia". The body functions are more able to aid in combating hypothermia when given assistance at 37°C or 36°C than at lower temperatures, as more body functions are still operative and able to assist in the process of accepting outside help to produce inner core warmth. The faster you are at diagnosis and the quicker you are at getting treatment underway the better it will be for the victim.

Just as there are three stages to hypothermia, Early Warning Signs, Mild Hypothermia and Profound Hypothermia, there are three sets of guidelines for treatment, one for each stage, almost as if there were three distinct illnesses.

Assessing the Situation

If medical treatment can be reached in one hour, move toward that goal without making camp, provided you have diagnosed the problem in its early stages.

If the decision is to reach assistance within one hour, provide help to the victim. Urge him or her to keep walking, which will help to maintain warmth. Carry the victim's pack, offer sweetened water and increase insulation against the cold. Support him or her while walking and encourage progress, but do not rush. See "Treating Early Signs of Hypothermia".

If reaching medical treatment will take more than one hour, or if hypothermia is advanced, you must stop, make camp and proceed with field treatment immediately. Achieve some additional insulation, wind protection and heat supply within fifteen minutes, and full effective treatment as quickly as possible. Organize for the necessary assistance to move the victim to civilization as soon as you have the manpower available to do so. This might include seeking outside help through warning flares, S.O.S. banners, beacon fires by night, smoke fires by day or sending a rested party out of camp for help. See "Treating Mild Hypothermia in the Field".

If assistance is unavailable and an attempt must be made in the field to treat the victim, follow the procedures as listed. Take care to warm the victim's inner core in a gentle fashion to avoid medical complications with the heart rhythm and acidosis: oxygen shortage in tissues because the cold heart is overworked and cannot pump enough oxygenated blood to peripheral areas that have been warmed too early in the treatment. When the victim has regained body core warmth, then more attention may be paid to peripheral areas. See "Treating Mild and Profound Hypothermia in the Field".

While assessing the situation, check the condition of other members of the group, keep them active, so they don't cool too much until nourished and protected from the cold. Do not exhaust them before they have time to rest. Take turns for rest and rest regularly under protection from the environment.

Basic Rules for Treating Hypothermia in the Field

The basic rules for treating hypothermia in the field, apply to all stages of the illness. However, these rules may be applied in varying ways, depending on whether the person suffering from the illness is ambulatory, cooperative and resting, mentally or physically unable to cooperate, or unconscious. You will find suggestions on how to apply these rules in the rest of this chapter. Memorize these *basic rules*. Use them and the suggestions herein, to make the best decisions you can in the circumstances that confront you, if you are ever involved in a hypothermic emergency. Appendix A contains a summary of this chapter.

Memorize this list

1. Be gentle, be quick and cause the victim to rest.
2. Protect the victim from cold, wind and rain.
3. Remove all wet and perspiration-damp clothing. Get victim into dry clothing or an alternative dry covering such as blankets or a sleeping bag.
4. Insulate from further heat loss by wrapping the victim in blankets, or alternatives. Place a warm hat on his head.
5. Take special care to apply warmth in those areas containing vital organs: head, neck, armpits, chest and groin.
6. If victim is still conscious (and can swallow) and has no violent spasms of shivering: reduce dehydration and improve energy by offering sweet warm drinks. No coffee, no alcohol and no smoking.

Anytime you are faced with a hypothermic situation think first of your basic rules, then proceed with treatment, keeping in mind the four ways the body loses heat: radiation, conduction, convection and evaporation.

Treating Early Warning Signs of Hypothermia

With immediate care to reduce further heat loss and stress on the victim, you may be able to proceed to safety without stopping to make camp; provided the distance is not too great or the weather conditions too difficult. If you feel you must stop and make camp, refer to the outline in the next section on mild hypothermia. The following points outline a course of action for ambulatory patients.

1. Stop heat loss by replacing all damp clothing with dry clothing. If you have a survival blanket wrap this around the victim's torso under their outer clothing. Increase the insulation around the body by adding extra clothes or creating a shawl from a blanket or sleeping bag to place around the victim's head and body. If you have no extra insulation for the victim, provide the victim with a windproof covering such as rainwear or plastic sheeting, secured against flapping in the air. Do not stop for too long a time period while making these adjustments. You must avoid too much chilling inactivity.

2. Reduce the energy requirements of the victim by carrying his or her equipment, and letting the victim lean on you for support.

3. Move at the victim's pace. Move directly towards safety, foregoing all other plans for the outing.

4. Improve the energy reserves of the victim (and the whole group) by giving them carbohydrates in an easily assimilated form such as warm sweet drinks and candy.

5. Rest often with short rests, insulated from the ground and out of the wind.

6. Watch for deterioration in the victim and in all members of the group. Be prepared to stop and make camp if the situation warrants it.

Treating Mild Hypothermia in the Field

The circumstances of every case of hypothermia are different. The purpose of this detailed list is to give you some ideas for treatment, when treatment must be given in a temporary campsite. It is up to you to recognize which ideas will suit your situation and equipment. If you suspect mild hypothermia or early warning signs of hypothermia in a member of your group, no matter how slight the symptoms are, act quickly and with complete care, for the fact that you have stopped on the trail at all may further cool the victim and increase hypothermia. As time, number and condition of companions allows, act on all aspects of protection from heat loss, for the victim and for the whole group, in an organized fashion doing the most important things first.

1. Don't waste time choosing the perfect campsite. Take the best that's at hand for a sheltered spot and start treatment, as shown in the list of *Basic Rules* and in Appendix A.

2. Add a tent or bivouac, a fire or heating stove and other improvements as soon as the group can respond to these needs.

3. If wet clothing cannot be replaced with dry clothing immediately, encase the victim in plastic sheeting (except for the face) or rubberized rainwear to inhibit evaporation, then wrap the person in blankets, sleeping bags, etc. until dried clothing is available.

4. If a survival blanket is available wrap it around the victim over the dry clothing but under the extra insulating layers, making sure to protect the head, neck, chest and groin areas from further cooling. As soon as safe heat is available (heat that can be tolerated on the skin or clothing, depending on how it is to be utilized) apply it to the groin and armpits, core areas where the blood vessels are close to the skin, and around the head, neck and chest. (See Chapter 6.)

For years, treatment of hypothermia included warming the victim by contact with other naked companions inside a sleeping bag. This, however, is not the best way to warm the victim, as too much heat is lost in the process of stripping and getting organized. Many sleeping bags are simply not big enough to accommodate two or three people. If you have no other source of heat and this form of warming must be used, do not strip the victim or warm companion completely. Leave on the hats and all dry inner clothing of both parties. Exchange any damp clothing they have for dry clothing.

5. Do not try to heat arms and legs and frozen areas. Cover these areas with dry clothing and wrap them in blankets to insulate against the cold and prevent further heat loss. Keep frozen areas insulated against premature warming until medical treatment is available.

6. Do not encourage activity in arms or legs of the victim

or do anything that will encourage circulation, such as rubbing the arms or legs. Increased blood flow in these cold areas is not desirable at this time.

7.   Insulate the body in a horizontal position with the feet slightly elevated and head level, thereby encouraging circulation of blood to the body inner core and brain.

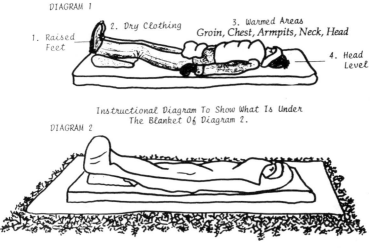

DIAGRAM 1

2. *Dry Clothing*
1. *Raised Feet*
3. *Warmed Areas*
Groin, Chest, Armpits, Neck, Head
4. *Head Level*

Instructional Diagram To Show What Is Under The Blanket Of Diagram 2.

DIAGRAM 2

5.   *Apply maximum insulation for the victim - using a warm hat, blankets, sleeping bag, campers mattress, groundsheet and compressed material such as boughs or snow.*

6.   *Heat the air around the victim in the shelter.*

Six Important Points of Care for a Victim of Hypothermia

8.   Separate the body from the ground to protect against moisture and cold. Use a ground sheet or floor of the tent, plus whatever you have at hand for insulation: sleeping bags, foamy, air mattress etc, or natural insulation. (See Chapter 6.)

9.   Heat the environment within your sheltered area so that the air being breathed by the victim is warm. Having other people in the shelter will help to warm and moisturize the air, as well as share the whole group's limited heat production. (See Chapter 6.)

10.   If the victim is conscious and can swallow (test by placing a drop of water on the victim's tongue, then watching the Adam's apple for a swallowing movement) and has no

violent spasms of shivering, offer the victim something sweet to drink. Heat the drink to a modest 43°C (lukewarm). The actual heat of the drink does not add measurably to the inner core temperature of the victim, but it is useful against dehydration and can aid energy reserves when sugar or syrup has been added. Psychologically, a warm drink is supportive, although experience shows the victim often asks for cold water and should be given what he asks for. Avoid using a metal cup, as it might be too hot for the victim's lips. Hold the cup when the victim is drinking as clumsy hands may drop the cup, adding additional moisture to the clothing. No alcohol, no coffee, no smoking.

Smoking and coffee increase stress to the body. Alcohol disrupts the normal thermoregulation of the nervous systems. The somatic nervous system gives the brain false messages of security and warmth. The autonomic nervous system becomes slow to initiate the measures needed to protect the body from further cooling. At the same time the cardiovascular system in the body dilates. This floods the skin with blood, accounting for the false warm feeling from the alcohol. This cooled blood then returns to cool the body inner core, increasing the degree of hypothermia.

11. The victim may want to urinate frequently. Use a pot or a bottle to assist him or her, avoid excessive movement and prevent wetting of the clothes.

12. If the victim is experiencing major difficulty breathing, assist ventilation with mouth-to-mouth resuscitation. This helps the victim's overtaxed lungs to gain oxygen from your preheated and moisturized breath at a time when the victim can least afford to take in cold air.

13. As the victim improves, additional sweets may be given, however, proteins and fats place too much stress on the digestive system. Slowly increase warmth, nutrients and water while monitoring the patient at all times. Insist on absolute rest to make sure there is no set back until pulse, coloring, warmth and the patient's five senses are fully recovered.

14. If victim does not seem to be improving, increase

your diligence in all precautions to reduce loss of body heat and continue to warm the head, neck, chest, armpits and groin areas. Be very gentle and treat for profound hypothermia. Your patient is in very serious trouble and must have medical attention immediately!

15. If assistance comes, move the victim with extreme care. Use a stretcher or as much assistance as you can give, to complete the move to safety gently, with as little stress and chilling as possible.

Treating Profound Hypothermia in the Field

Your patient is gravely ill. When shivering ceases, the body's inner core temperature is down to 32°C and unconsciousness will soon result. Medical help is necessary!

Follow all of the procedures named in the above sections with the exception of administering drink and food. Food and drink would further chill the body's inner core and the victim has lost the ability to swallow. You must do the best you can, keeping these thoughts in mind:

1. Be very gentle.

2. Avoid moving the victim before medical direction arrives, if at all possible.

3. If the victim regains consciousness, keep him or her warm and quiet.

4. Continue mouth-to-mouth resuscitation, or an alternate supply of warm moistened air to breathe. Continue all methods of care aimed at warming the body's inner core.

5. Don't assume death because you cannot find a pulse or see breathing. At these temperatures the victim will show few signs of life.

6. Do not give up as long as you are safe yourself, as there may still be a spark of life. Any medical facility will not pronounce death until the body has been returned to an acceptable inner core temperature, just in case life still exists.

7. If you have success, do not hurry the warming process

too much to avoid acidosis and heart stress.

8. Find medical attention and hospitalization. Your patient must continue to be thoroughly insulated, both from the cold and from premature warming of peripheral areas or frozen parts until hospitalization or medical services take over the case. The victim must be lifted and transported with extreme care.

Conclusions and Recommendations

Be gentle. Be quick. Think about insulation and body core physiology in warming the victim. Create a warm, dry resting place away from the wind, for the victim and the rest of the group. With the *Basic Rules* for treating hypothermia committed to memory and the knowledge of *how the body loses heat*, you should be able to treat hypothermia successfully under most circumstances, provided you have diagnosed the illness in reasonable time and planned ahead to have the right equipment with you. For a quick reference list for treatment of hypothermia, refer to Appendix A.

Part C
Wilderness Skills

Wood and Water, Wind and Tree
Wisdom, Strength, and Courtesy,
Jungle-Favour go with thee!

Rudyard Kipling
(1865-1936)
The Mowgli Stories

Hypothermia is not selective. It may occur on the prairies, in the bush, on rocky seashores or in thick forest. Every season and geographical area requires camping skills unique to its own topography and weather conditions, and the reader must apply logic on how to implement the theory to conditions present, when faced with the dangers of hypothermia. People experienced with the outdoors may know many of these skills, however, reviewing them may refresh your memory in the way they pertain to protecting yourself from hypothermia through effective planning and wilderness skills.

5

Effective Planning for Protection Against Hypothermia

The plans made for protection against cold weather before leaving home may save your life. The body needs energy and protection from wind, moisture and cold for survival. The plans made must satisfy these needs when planning the food to take, the clothes needed, the equipment carried for a shelter, and the provision for making heat. Making effective plans requires information on many aspects of the trip. The season, the topography, the length and difficulty of the trip, and the proficiencies and strengths of every member of the group, make the planning unique for each trip. After the initial planning is completed, you will need to determine whether it is physically possible to carry all the things that seem important to take and establish priorities to reduce the load if necessary. Effective planning correlates priority needs with reasonable backpack weight restrictions.

The Nutritional Significance in Planning Food for the Wilderness

The foods to take on an outing must have sufficient calories to supply the energy requirements of everyone in the group. They should be high in carbohydrates and easy to digest. In choosing foods for the menus look for lightweight products (low in moisture content), with good keeping qualities, easy preparation, and compact packaging.

Calorie Requirements for Energy

The following exercise will teach you a great deal about menu planning and lightweight foods of greatest benefit on a wilderness trip. Plan a menu in your usual fashion and then using a Calorie table for foods, determine the total Calories you are taking on your trip and compare it to the following general rule:

A full day of hiking for the average adult of 160 pounds will require 3 000 to 3 500 Calories.

Scale this number up or down depending on the weight of the hikers in the group, the difficulty of the trip, the cold that might be encountered and extra activities planned for the trip (swimming, rappelling, etc.). Multiply the daily Calorie requirements of the group by the number of days planned for the trip. Add an additional allotment of Calories for emergencies, depending on the scale of your outing and distance from civilization.

For example:
The Calories needed by 4 hikers weighing 140, 160, 160 and 180 pounds on a summer hike for three days would be approximately:

$$1 \text{ (hiker) x } \frac{140}{160} \text{ x } 3\,000 \approx 2\,625 \text{ Calories}$$

$$2 \text{ (hikers) x } \frac{160}{160} \text{ x } 3\,000 \approx 6\,000 \text{ Calories}$$

$$1 \text{ (hiker) x } \frac{180}{160} \text{ x } 3\,000 \approx 3\,375 \text{ Calories}$$

---

12 000 x 3 days

36 000 Calories

The Calorie requirements for the Day-1 breakfast and the Day-3 supper should be included, even though they are to be eaten before and after the trip. This will allow for the extra Calories required for emergency rations.

If the trip is to be more strenuous use 3 500 Calories instead of 3 000 per person. If the trip is to be in winter weather use up to 4 000 per day per person. Working with this guide you should have adequate provisions when starting the trip. If the bulk and weight of these provisions are too great to carry, you must find replacement foods for the menu that conserve packaging, weight and fluid content. Do not start your trip with inadequate food supplies.

Nutritional Content of Foods
Commonly Used for Outdoor Menus

The following is a list of some foods, commonly found in hiking menus, divided into three categories.

In planning against hypothermia it is important to recognize the difference between carbohydrates, proteins and fats. Although foods are often a combination of the three elements, they have been divided into categories based on the nutrient of major importance in that food.

Foods Noted for:

Carbohydrates	Protein	Fat
Sugar	Canned or	Cooking Oil
Candy	Dehydrated:	Butter
Jam and Peanut Butter	Meats	Margarine
Syrup	Fish	Lard
Sweet Drinks	Poultry	Bacon (not
Dextrose Tablets	Eggs	recommended
Instant Puddings	Milk	for bear country)
Jelly Powders	Lentils	Nuts
Cookies	Soy Bean	Cheese
Cake Mix	Products	Peanut Butter
Bread	Navy Beans	Canned and Pressed
Flour	Cheese	Meats
Pasta	Peanut Butter	Tuna and Sardines
Rice	Nuts	packed in oil
Oatmeal	Beef Jerky	
Pita Bread		
Pancake Mix		
Baking Powder		
Biscuit Mix		
Fresh Fruit and		
Vegetables:		
Apples		
Oranges		
Carrots		
Dried Fruit:		
Raisins		
Apricots		
Prunes		
Figs		
Peaches		
"Fruit Roll-Ups"		
Fruit Drink Powders		
Instant Potatoes		
Dehydrated Vegetables		
Powdered Soup Mixes		

Carbohydrates, Proteins and Fats as Related to Hypothermia

Carbohydrates:
- are easily digested.
- supply immediate energy.

    – should be the major portion of the food supply.

    – are very important as snacks along the trail.

Proteins:

    – are more difficult to digest.

    – do not supply much immediate energy.

    – repair wear and tear on the body, therefore the longer the duration of the camping period, the more important it is that they be regularly included in the menu.

Fats:

    – are more difficult to digest.

    – give some immediate energy.

    – are important to many body functions and should be included in the menu at meals.

The intake of proteins and fats should be at meal times, followed by a rest period of one to two hours, depending on the amount of fat and protein in the meal. This rest period allows the natural responses of the body to divert blood circulation to the digestive system, which aids in proper digestion and function of the bowels. High activity after a meal needing digestion time for fat and protein jeopardizes either digestion, defecation or muscular activity.

Plan for a good breakfast before starting out each day, followed by a rest period or time of light activity, such as checking maps, bird watching or local nature appreciation. Plan for the the heaviest meal at night, followed by a good night's sleep.

Trail Snacks

Frequent snacks of high energy food along the trail will sustain your energy level and help combat fatigue and hypothermia. Hard candy made with sugar is a carbohydrate and very suitable for trail snacks. Chocolate bars are another favorite high energy snack but they melt in the sun and in warm pockets, and are very hard in the cold weather, which makes them difficult to bite on. Bite-sized chocolate, such as Rosebuds and chocolate chips, are best for cold weather. Chocolate bars and candy particularly suited for high energy are sold at most camping supply stores.

A homemade mixture of small hard candies, nuts and

dried fruit, universally called Gorp, supplies high energy and a trace of protein and fat for an acceptable compliment of nutritives for a trail snack. Each hiker should make a bag of mix according to taste for each day of the trip. This bag should be sized to fit in a pocket for easy access along the trail. A favorite combination is three-flavor after-dinner mints, salted peanuts, sunflower seeds, raisins, dried apricots and dried prunes. Chewing on the dried apricots and prunes or sucking the prune pit are effective ways to keep the mouth moist and comfortable while hiking and cross-country skiing.

Dextra-Sol is a high energy tablet, very light and compact with long keeping qualities. It is suitable for your first aid kit, in treatment of shock and hypothermia (If the patient can swallow). Carry it for emergencies in your backpack and car.

Vitamins and Minerals

Hiking menus are often low in some important vitamins and minerals because of the absence of fresh fruit and vegetables, and dairy products. If your regular eating habits are good and your diet is nutritionally balanced with adequate vitamins and minerals, your body will have a vitamin reserve. If your regular food habits are poor, or you are not aware of vitamin requirements, you could easily start out on your venture in poor condition, allowing very little back-up in your system for the stress of hypothermia.

On an extended trip you should consider taking standard vitamin and mineral tablets. This would protect your ability to heal small cuts and scrapes, maintain night vision, reduce fatigue and irritability, and generally help digestion and metabolism. Despite the restrictions encountered in hiking menus, do your best to plan a menu that will continue to be balanced and nutritious. Dried apricots, prunes, raisins, peanuts, sunflower seeds, canned pork, soybean products, vitamin C fortified juice mixes, powdered eggs and milk, oatmeal and whole grain products will all add to the vitamin content of your meals.

The mineral of prime importance while hiking is salt. Salt is easily flushed from the body through excessive perspiration during periods of high activity or during hot weather.

Symptoms of low salt include extreme fatigue and aching or cramping muscles. This fatigue might limit your ability to complete wilderness plans before nightfall, providing exposure to hypothermia in the cool night temperatures. When experiencing periods of high perspiration, include a little salt in the menu, i.e., salted peanuts or salt with the food. This should be sufficient salt to protect body functions. If the environment is very hot and your perspiration profuse, one salt tablet taken with adequate water to replace fluid losses, will provide the desired relief from fatigue.

Safe Adequate Fluids

Water is often the most refreshing drink while on the trail, with tea, coffee, cocoa and fruit drinks at rest periods or meals. Do not drink alcohol. Alcohol depresses activity in the central nervous system, subverts normal thermoregulation of the body, and increases heat loss through the skin.

Daily Fluid Requirements

The daily minimum fluid requirement for an adult under normal conditions is two litres of fluid per day. In outdoor conditions, even more fluid intake is needed to replenish fluid lost through evaporation, perspiration and increased urination (caused from increased muscular activity). Hikers cannot begin to carry this amount of fluid in their packs, nor can they assume they will find suitable water on the trail. All natural waters from lakes, rivers, rain or snow in civilized areas and the wilderness must be assumed to have pollutants. Serious illnesses such as giardia (beaver feaver), worms and enteroviruses, (intestinal disorders causing cramps, diarrhea or constipation) can come from these waters. Don't take chances. Plan to purify drinking water.

Purifying Natural Water

Choose natural water from the best source available. Running water is better than stagnant water. The farther from shore, the better the water in a lake. Melt fresh snow rather than dip from snow-melt puddles. Catch fresh rain water. Avoid glacial run-off streams and rivulets. The "rock flour" (finely ground rock) held in suspension in these waters can be irritating to the digestive tract and may cause cramps. If you must use glacial run-off, dip it from quiet settling pools. Strain visible impurities from water before treatment and again after treatment if impurities settle out in the bottom of your container. Be prepared to purify any natural waters before use. There are two accepted inexpensive ways for purifying water: boiling and iodination. Chlorine base water purification tablets and bleach are not effective against all pollutants and are no longer considered acceptable.

To treat water by boiling, it must be boiled to a full rolling boil for twenty minutes to render it safe for drinking. This may appear to be a simple method of treatment, but it is difficult to boil water for twenty minutes without losing the major portion of the water to evaporation, to say nothing of fuel consumption in a lightweight stove or the work of stoking a fire for that length of time.

Iodination of water is a process for purifying water using Iodine as the active ingredient. It is considered the safest method of water purification found within the requirements of the outdoor person: the materials can be carried in a lightweight purifying kit, the process is easy to use, fast acting, palatable, and effective in hot, cold or freezing, alkaline or acidic water. It can also be regulated to treat particularly polluted water. (People treated for hyperthyroidism should check with a doctor before using this product.)

Water purification by iodination can be achieved three ways: commercial tablet form, iodine crystals or Tincture of Iodine (2.5% in ethanol). Not all pharmacists or camping stores regularly carry some of these products so it would be best to place your order ahead of time to be sure of availability.

Tablets provide a simple straight forward method of purification, however, the tablet is subject to losing some of its effectiveness with storage and even more once the container has been opened. Follow the directions on the container. Brand names include "Globaline", sold in the United States, and "Puritabs" made by Kirby Pharmaceuticals and used by the Canadian army.

Iodine crystals can be carried in your first aid kit and used about 1 000 times. With the crystals, the pharmacist will provide you with a 30 ml glass bottle and instructions for the iodination procedure. The procedure involves making a water solution in the small bottle using the iodine crystals, and using the solution in treating the strained natural waters. Treatment takes about fifteen minutes, or forty minutes with a weaker solution designed to have a better flavor. Most campers find the fifteen minute process acceptable. The iodine crystals are highly toxic and must not be eaten. One kit sold by camping stores has the brand name "Polarpure".

Tincture of Iodine is available in either the regular orange color or the decolorized form. Use eight drops to 1 litre or 1 quart of water and let stand one hour. This method is noted for its strong iodine flavor.

Treated water should be poured back and forth or shaken to add air to the water and improve the flavor. Orange crystals may be added to improve the flavor. Store treated water in a closed clean container. If no other way of purifying natural water sources is available, at the very least strain and boil the water before drinking it.

The tablets are the easiest of the above named processes to use, but the crystals may be the best long term addition to your first aid kit.

Planning for Protective Clothing

Your first protection against cold is the insulating quality of your clothing. Many fabrics lose up to 90% of their insulating qualities when they become damp from perspiration or wet from the environment. Ask your camping store about new fabrics. Apart from these new fabrics, wool is one of the best fabrics for warmth, wet or dry. Cotton is one of the worst fabrics when wet, yet how many hikers continue to wear cotton blue jeans.

Wear long pants and a long-sleeved shirt for all weather, even in the summer. This will also help to protect you from insect bites, poison ivy and scratches. The warmer the weather, the lighter the *fabric* worn.

If the weather is so warm that shorts or cut offs are your preference, be aware that you are taking the risk of wasting energy. Be prepared to change into long trousers as soon as you sense the slightest amount of cooling.

Choose a wardrobe that will fit the variety of conditions that could be encountered on your trip. Dress in layers of clothing, adding layers when resting and removing layers when active. Suit the layers of clothing to the heat of the day and your amount of activity to stay sufficiently warm but never perspiring. Sweaters and jackets with front openings make it easier to control heat build up. If you are warm because of high activity, removing layers of clothing will allow you to be more comfortable, however, if you are concerned about perspiring and wasting energy you would be wiser to reduce your rate of high activity.

Have outer layers of clothing larger than inner layers to allow for suitable air space between the layers and improve their insulating qualities. Keep in mind that tighter weaves of cloth and tighter stitches in knitting withstand wind better than loose weaves and open knitting, and that the new lighter weight fabrics take less energy to carry on your back and in your pack than heavier weight fabrics.

Include a hat, facial protection, mitts and extra socks in your kit. Have good quality rain gear (or alternatively good quality snow gear more suitable for cold) that covers all of your body; legs, feet, hands and head. Ponchos are not suitable for rain except to tie down over your pack and serve as a ground sheet. They are too easily ruffled by wind, allowing in moisture and cold.

If you have all your warm clothing on and are still cold, add something that will stop the wind, such as a plastic garbage bag, sheet of plastic or rain gear. Always travel with a sheet of builder's plastic or large garbage bag in your kit. Include a sit-upon in the gear: a square of insulite. Insulite is a special kind of foam padding that offers both insulation from cold and protection from ground moisture and is available at any hostel shop or camping store.

Planning for Protective Shelter

Different types of outings need planning unique to that outing. Duration of the trip, distance and the degree of cold expected, will vary your plans for protective shelter.

The Survival Blanket

A good safety kit on the trail and in your vehicle should include a survival blanket. The survival blanket is the lightest and easiest way to assure yourself of a simple shelter in an emergency. It is the size of a normal blanket yet only the weight and size of an envelope when folded up. It has a silvered surface that reflects heat rays from the body, back toward the body in an efficient way to reduce body heat loss. In the treatment of hypothermia it is invaluable for conserving the victim's limited heat reserves. The survival blanket can be purchased in two styles, reusable and disposable, at a hostel shop or camping store. Carrying a survival blanket on a day trip in moderate weather is likely adequate shelter in the event of an emergency. It represents the minimum "shelter" to take on a day outing.

Overnight Shelter

If an overnight excursion is planned, have a good lightweight tent as well as a survival blanket. The tent should be storm proof with a floor and anti-weather fly or double walls. You must have the ability to set it up on the ground conditions which will be encountered. Gravel, earth and snow all require different types of pegs or mechanisms to tie the tent down. If a tent is not available or extra protection is desired, consider taking a large sheet of builder's plastic and some light cord to snug the plastic down over bushes, poles or a cliff for support or act as a ground sheet. An axe and/or saw and light cord are almost mandatory and are needed in building a shelter from natural materials without undue exertion.

Your choice of shelter may vary, but whatever you choose, make a conscious effort to plan ahead for protective shelter.

Planning for the Ability to Make Heat

Never go into the wilderness without a means to make heat! Be aware that matches alone are not always trustworthy in rain, wind or cold because they cannot generate enough heat in their short life to warm the combustible material sufficiently to make it burst into flame. Matches must be complimented with tools for working with firewood. Sufficient firewood is not easy to collect without an axe or saw. Saws are more energy efficient in cutting logs than an axe. Hostel shops and camping stores sell lightweight compact tools.

Matches

Every camper should carry a supply of matches, and this supply divided in at least two different locations (in a pocket and in the pack, for example). Wooden matches burn three times longer than paper matches, allowing more time to heat the combustible material while trying to light it. Keep the matches in a sealed container so they can't draw humidity from the air. The container must be easy to open with cold, wet or gloved fingers. Carry something that lights easily, such as fire starting cubes, flammable paste or a lightweight stove. In addition to matches, a reliable "Zippo" lighter containing liquid lighter fluid, and kept in a pocket near body heat, will usually light in cold weather, and produces a continuous flame.

Lightweight Stoves

Lightweight stoves use butane, propane, alcohol or naptha. They all have limitations in cold and altitude.

Butane is useless in temperatures nearing and below freezing. Butane, in its liquid state (in the pressurized bomb), freezes at 0°C prohibiting vaporization and the ability to light. Altitude increases the problems with butane, not only because with sufficient altitude there is reduced oxygen, causing difficulty lighting it in borderline temperatures, but because environmental temperatures decrease with altitude. A stove that works in your base camp might not work on the mountain in cold weather.

Propane is difficult to light in temperatures nearing -25 °C, with its liquid state freezing at -40 °C. Altitude increases this difficulty. As winter storms could easily drop to these temperatures propane has limited trustworthiness in the winter.

Alcohol, as it is a liquid, will light in winter and in altitude; however, it burns with such low heat production that extreme cold will sap most of the available heat produced. This renders it ineffective as a heat source in the stove or in producing a flame with sufficient heat to start a campfire.

Naphtha (white gas) must vaporize to light. In cold conditions this will not occur in a stove without a pressure pump, thus making it useless. If the stove has a pressure pump, you will be able to make it light if you can warm the gas chamber sufficiently to start vaporizing the naphtha. This is usually done in ordinary conditions by leaking a little naphtha into the gas chamber and lighting it. If this proves too difficult, leak the naphtha into a small container, place the container in the heart of your unlit campfire and then light the gas carefully. Use the campfire to increase the temperature around the stove, and then try to light the stove in the regular way. Extreme care must be taken as all of these procedures are dangerous, specially with your heavy clothing limiting your movements. Do not spill naphtha on the campfire and light it. This is a dangerous practice and it might not concentrate the heat under your unlit campfire sufficiently to light it. It is also more wasteful of your precious fuel.

Propane stoves are likely the safest stove for spring, summer and fall, but not sufficiently trustworthy for winter conditions. Naphtha stoves are likely the best in winter as naphtha can be used as a fire starter and once warmed, the stove will work. However, it would be safer to use flammable paste or fire starting cubes for starting the campfire to be used in warming the stove.

No matter which source of heat is chosen, practice with it in cold and rain before leaving home! Be sure it will function under the conditions which might be faced.

Conclusions and Recommendations

Consumables contribute immensely to your health and feeling or well-being. Understand them and plan balanced menus with adequate Calories for your trip. Always purify your drinking water. Keep wind, moisture and cold in mind when planning your wardrobe and your shelter. Never go into the wilderness without testing your ability to make heat, in the same circumstances you will be encountering on your trip.

6

Camping Skills for Protection against Hypothermia

Useful camping skills for protection against hypothermia are those that protect you from moisture, wind and cold. Choosing your campsite, erecting shelter, building a fire and managing to stay dry are all important. Unfortunately, the best laid plans do not cover all situations and your survival may depend on your ability to find assistance from nature's provisions. Although teaching survival this book does not condone "survival camping" (needless destruction of the environment just for the challenge). In a hypothermic emergency you seldom face ideal conditions, and it is hoped that the following suggestions may present ideas that will help in your situation.

Choosing a Campsite

When confronted with hypothermia there will be insufficient time to search for the ideal campsite. You must make do with what is at hand. Make the decision for the location and do the best possible to provide protection from cold, wind and moisture. The following considerations might be useful in making that decision.

Avoid building your campsite at the bottom of the valley or at the water's edge. Just as water chooses to collect in the low contours of the land, so does cold air. Make camp part way up the hill, above the layer of cold air, but not so far up the hill that you find more wind turbulence.

Avoid contours of land where wind tunnels are formed. Try to use natural protection of vegetation, hills and cliffs to locate still air. Know the prevailing winds of the area in choosing your sheltered spot. Position your campsite to allow for protection from the most expected changes of wind directions.

Make the most out of heat from the sun. In cold weather never sit in the shade if you can be in the sun. Make the most of morning sun in your campsite. If possible, place the shelter on the northwest side of a small clearing, facing the sunrise yet still seeking maximum wind protection.

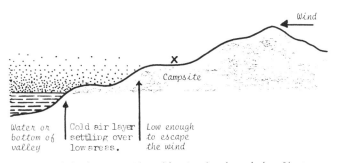

Contours of land representing old water levels and shorelines.

Locating the campsite

Erecting a Shelter

To treat hypothermia effectively in a temporary campsite a shelter is essential to permit heating of the air, reducing the chilling of the body. If a tent is not available, then a shelter must be made from items carried with the equipment, supplemented by items found in nature nearby. Consider the following suggestions.

Locating the Shelter

As the fire will be built immediately in front of the opening of the shelter you must consider where it will be safe to build a fire in conjunction with where you position the shelter. Place the tent or bivouac with the door at 90° to the wind for minimal smoke in the shelter and maximum radiated heat from the fire. See the diagrams showing the best juxtaposition for the shelter, fire, woodpile and wind direction on pages 73-76.

The shelter must not be in a low spot. Position the shelter on a mound or slightly sloping ground, so moisture will drain away.

Environmental Insulation

Different natural surfaces provide distinctive qualities of insulation against environmental cold. Consider the surface on which your tent is placed or where you sit.

Rock may be dry but it is as cold as the environmental temperature. i.e., at -20°C, rock will also be -20°C.

Frozen earth is a little warmer, but almost as cold as rock.

Wood has less ability to transfer heat from your body and offers some insulation qualities when placed between the body and ground or snow.

Snow has a temperature a little below freezing and therefore offers quite a lot of insulation when coping with weather below freezing. Generally, 15 centimeters of packed snow are needed to give relief from cold ground temperatures. To use snow effectively, a moisture and heat barrier must be in place. The floor of the tent, a poncho, or a sheet of plastic will serve as a moisture barrier. A heavy log across the opening of the tent or bivouac will prevent the heat radiated by the fire from melting the snow packed under the floor of your shelter.

A matting of branches incorporates air spaces for additional insulation, and can be used as an insulation over your body as well as under it. Matting can be made of compressed twigs, evergreen boughs, moss, dry grass, reeds and dry pine needles. If the matting is moist or from green cuttings, it is better if you have the tent floor or plastic on top of it for a moisture barrier. Such a matting should be at least 4 centimetres thick after compression. The insulation provided by a matting of branches will also act as a partial moisture barrier between snow and a sleeping bag.

In winter the best insulation would be to locate your tent or bivouac on snow, covered with a matting of sticks or boughs, which in turn is covered with the tent floor or groundsheet, foamy and sleeping bag, giving added insulation for your body. The important thing is to get the shelter up and in use, then add the branches or boughs for extra insulation, as you have time and energy.

Building the Shelter

Shelters can be constructed to form an open lean-to or an enclosed structure like a wigwam with a smoke hole in the roof. Enclosed shelters require less heat to keep them warm, but have a terrible smoke problem if you have to rely on a fire for heat. An open lean-to can be kept warm but consumes vast amounts of firewood. Nature will dictate your abilities in building the shelter by the construction materials available and the amount of burnable material at hand. If you have to build a shelter, a large sheet of plastic is very useful against wind and moisture. Do your best to snug the plastic down over supports to create an area of still air, and over the floor of the shelter for a moisture barrier. Building a shelter is hard work. Do not get overheated and damp from perspiration.

Design features of enclosed or open shelters are similar in the construction of the floors and walls. The enclosed shelter is more useful if you can heat it with hot rocks or a stove to avoid the smoke problem. Assure adequate ventilation for fumes if using a stove. Design features of an open shelter should start with a maximum height of about one and two-thirds metres. This gives the roof enough height to trap the heat from the fire, yet, it is still low enough that all of the warmed air, which you need for relief against hypothermia, is not over your head. The shelter must not be too deep or the heat radiated from the fire will not warm its cavernous interior. Plan the fire area in conjunction with the shelter plans.

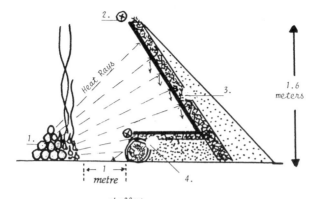

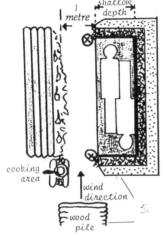

Under adverse conditions there is no such thing as a perfect shelter. Do the best you can.

1. Heat reflectors for the fire should run the full length of the shelter. In moderate temperatures the leading edge of the fire should be 1 metre from the front of the shelter: 2/3 that distance when temperatures are below 0°C.

2. Wind and moisture barrier (x to x) in the roof and floor of the shelter if you have something you can use in your equipment.

3. Insulation gained from branches layered over supporting poles for the back wall and ends of the shelter, covered with more branches or snow.

4. Insulation in the raised floor of the shelter, picturing 15 cm of packed snow covered by 4 cm of compacted twigs or boughs, protected from the fire by a large log.

5. Top view of the shelter designed for two, showing careful use of space and a safe, useful location for spare firewood.

Basic Measurements and Design of Shelters

Features of Shelters
Constructed from Natural Materials

1. The shelter is limited to the minimum size required by the occupants, so you are not heating extra space.
2. The floor of the shelter is raised above ground level, that is, above the coldest air, by adding as much insulation from compacted matting and snow as possible. The floor of the shelter should have a moisture barrier.
3. The leading edge of the compacted material, both matting and snow, must be protected from the fire by greenwood logs, rocks, earth, or sand to prevent the snow from melting or the matting from catching fire.
4. The walls must allow for controlled ventilation yet be as windproof as possible. Insulation can be enhanced by heaping more boughs and snow against the walls.
5. In constructing a snow shelter these same rules apply in the following ways. To obtain the maximum insulation from the snow against environmental cold, at least 15 cm of compacted snow is needed between you and the ground, as well as piled over the roof of the shelter. The resting bench must be complimented with a cold air well to drain cold air away from the bench. A hole in the roof of the structure will provide cross-ventilation with the entrance, where a little air should be allowed to enter. This hole may allow heat to escape, but with the passage of air will also remove carbon dioxide and moisture build-up. Before crawling into the shelter, securely "flag" the site with something bright like a towel, to attract searchers to the spot where you have taken refuge. This will reduce concern about being by-passed as just another snow drift. See the diagrams.

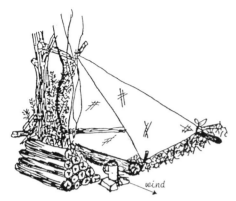

Wooded Area - Plastic Lean-To
    Fire Reflector - Greenwood Logs
    Matting Protector - Greenwood Log
    Matting - spruce boughs, twigs etc.

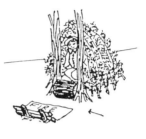

Wooded Area Single Bivouac
    Matting Protector - Large Log
    Insulation - 15 cms snow
        and matting

Rocky Area - Above the tree line or on a stoney river bank.
    Fire Reflector   - rocks
    Matting Protector - rocks
    Matting - grasses, small twigs

    Fire Reflector - soil from cave
    Matting protector - cliff face
    Matting - grasses, small twigs

Ideas for Shelters Constructed from Natural Materials and
Improved with Plastic Sheeting

SHELTER CONSTRUCTION   Continued

Bushland with willows and sandy soil.
Matting protection and reflector - soil.
Matting - twigs and live bushes.

Sleeping bench tunnelled into
a snow drift. Snowball or
pack for a door. Candle or
stove for heat. Ventilation
hole in the roof. Matting
of compressed twigs, boughs.

Step 1.
Dig a hole
with a
sleeping
bench, as
shown.

Step 2.
Cover sleeping bench
with matting and
arrange branches to support snow.

Small stove
or candle.

Step 3.
Spread groundsheet
over matting on
bench. A spare
groundsheet over
the supports before
adding snow will
keep the snow from melting
overhead and dripping through.
Ventilate the snow hump with a hole.

Matting

Sleeping
Bench

Cold Air Well

Climb in and try to heap the
snow over the hole.

Shelter Construction (continued)

The Ability to Make Heat

The fire must serve many purposes. It is for heat, drying clothes, warming water and food, warming rocks, heating the shelter where the victim is being treated, serving as a beacon and at night offering light. Consider your needs and your ability to obtain firewood; both the availability of wood and energy needed to collect it. Take care to save your energy and achieve the most relief with the smallest amount of work. Sawing down one or two trees nearby for firewood is far easier than trying to drag deadwood through undergrowth and snow to the site.

Heating the Shelter

In treating hypothermia, heat is necessary in the shelter. Initially, a tent may be heated with a lightweight stove or candles. Ultimately, a fire is needed to radiate heat into the shelter, for comfort and to conserve the other heat sources for better uses. If using a stove for heat, make sure the tent is well ventilated. A pot filled with hot rocks can also be used to heat a tent, and thus avoid the discomfort of smoke from a fire in an enclosed shelter. If this method of heating is used, raise the pot off the ground on perimeter supports to reduce loss of heat through conduction to the cold ground, and increase radiation of heat from all sides of the pot. Do not burn the floor of the tent with the hot pot. As hot air rises, tall tents need to have some of their height reduced so that the warm air near the roof can be breathed in a sitting position. If there is adequate firewood, heat radiated from a fire into the tent or open shelter provides the best way to warm an area for the group to rest and the hypothermia victim to be treated.

The fire must stretch the length of the opening into which the heat must be radiated, for adequate heat and prevention of cold areas in the shelter. Design a long narrow fire within one metre of the entrance to the shelter to achieve any success in radiating heat into it in conditions above freezing. In colder weather, reduce this distance by one third. Avoid locating the fire above major tree root systems, i.e., stay at least one and a half metres away from large trees. Before lighting the fire you must prepare the area where you intend to light the fire.

Scrape away leaves, twigs and other burnable debris, down to the ground. This is equally important in winter, if at all possible, as the melting snow will cause problems and the ground under the fire will get very hot and could start an underground fire along the root systems. Put the fire out when you leave, and disperse any hot rocks.

The Heat Reflector

The heat reflector should be about one metre high with the fire set along the front of it facing the shelter. The higher you can make the reflector the more heat reflected. The reflector should be running more or less parallel to the direction of the wind to reduce the smoke that circles back into the shelter.

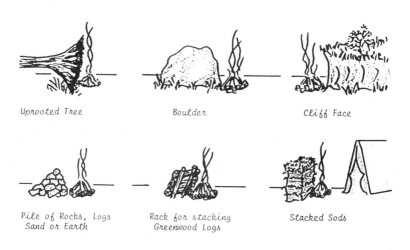

Uprooted Tree   Boulder   Cliff Face

Pile of Rocks, Logs   Rack for stacking   Stacked Sods
Sand or Earth   Greenwood Logs

The higher the reflector above the fire, the more heat will be reflected. In addition, the more acute the angle of the reflector, as in the tree root and for stacking logs, the more heat will be reflected.
Heat Reflectors

The reflector directing the heat of your fire into the shelter could be a stack of logs, piled rocks, stacked sods or piled earth. Your location might provide a cliff or rock face at a useful position to the wind for reflecting heat. You must do the best you can with what is at hand. If using logs for the reflector, green logs are better than dry wood, as they are slower to catch fire. More heat is reflected by a reflector sloping forward or vertical, than one sloping away from the fire.

Choice of Firewood and Lighting the Fire

Generally speaking, dead wood picked from standing trees is drier than wood found on the ground. Your initial fire must be made from very small dry twigs. When the fire is established, add larger sizes of wood until firewood is being used the size of your arm. Once a good bed of coals is established large logs and cold or green wood can be added. If further information about the various properties of firewood is desired, use a reference library; that information is too detailed for the general comments intended here. Stack enough wood in the woodpile to last easily through the night. The stack must be many times larger than the fire. It may look enormous but the supply will then not be depleted while the work force is asleep. Be sure to position the woodpile upwind from the fire for safety against having the wood pile catch on fire. Keep small sticks available in case the fire tries to die out and needs special attention. Organize sleeping arrangements to keep someone watching the fire and the patients all through the night.

When forced to build a fire in a hypothermic situation, making the fire light is often difficult. The theory for laying a fire and lighting it will work for any style of fire, although the following describes laying a fire for heat radiation into a shelter. You may find you have to get any type of small fire going for immediate needs and construct the larger fire and its reflector as time and energy permits.

Firewood, from twigs to large logs, will burn the best when laid diagonally upward in the path of a flame. This encourages the flame to travel along the wood for a short distance before regaining its upright nature, which gives the wood a longer exposure to the heat transferred by the flame, and more possibility of igniting when the wood is extremely cold. With small twigs and branches, the air space between the little sticks of firewood is also important. If the twigs are packed together too tightly there will not be enough oxygen for ignition. If there is too much air space the heat radiated from one burning stick to the next will not be great enough to expand the flames through the fire. Take a good handful of fine twigs 20 to 30 cm long and crack the bundle in the middle so they cling together in a compacted wad, giving a tee-pee effect. This diagonal line of the wad of twigs is ideal for your fire core. Always light the fire on the upwind side so that the little flames will reach into the fire as the wind carries them downwind.

Along the base of the reflector, make a long extension of compressed wads of twigs. Place larger sticks, about the size of your fingers, propped from the ground diagonally towards the reflector, over the twigs. Have larger wood ready to add to the fire immediately that you are sure the initial core is igniting. If your fire thrives you will soon be able to use logs as big as your arm and whole trees. Prepare a fire centre from the most flammable thing you can find such as dry paper, thin, dry layers of birch bark, dry birch or spruce twigs, spruce resin or all of these worked together. Make a hole for the fire centre in the fire core's small twigs at the upwind end of the fire. Once the fire centre is lit, the wind will help the fire to ignite through the core of twigs along the length of the whole reflector.

If difficulty is experienced in making the fire ignite, and no fire starter is available, such as flammable paste, or small stove, warm the matches and fire centre inside your shirt against the body before trying to light the fire. The wad of steel wool used to clean pots is excellent as a fire centre that lights easily. Light the initial fire centre at head height. The air is warmer at this height than on the ground and it is easier to blow gently into the ball of flammable material, coaxing it to burst into flame. When the flame is established, place the fire ball into the fire, in the hole prepared for it at the upwind end of the fire. Grasping the fire centre in pincers of wood may make holding the fire centre less dangerous, especially when wearing mitts.

A live fire this close to the shelter must be a controlled fire. The constant size of the fire should be just enough to be able to withstand the heat thrown the distance to the opening of the shelter. Control of the fire is gained through an effective wind-break (offered by the woodpile, stacked sods or other material), constant attention and the use of green wood in the reflector base if at all possible, or very large logs that will not burn through quickly.

Other Uses of the Fire

Cooking food or heating water is awkward and dangerous on a large fire with your movements hampered by heavy clothing. Organize a support for your pot, from rocks or heavy wood, upwind of the fire and scrape hot coals from your main fire into this "cooking area". If possible, prepare the support for your cooking pots before lighting the fire, when you can work closer to the fire area.

Hot rocks are very useful for transporting heat. They can be placed in wet socks, mitts, boots and clothing to speed up drying. Hot rocks can be carried into the shelter in a cooking pot for a source of heat, and turned out onto a log "hot pad". Small flat warmed rocks can be carried in jacket pockets as body warmers or wrapped in with the victim's blankets to warm the chest, neck, head and groin areas. The rocks can be any size: small enough to move to your campsite down to gravel and sand. All hold heat. Be very careful not to overheat rocks for your proposed use, as they can become very hot. Some sedimentary rocks are prone to cracking in heat or when suddenly chilled by cold water or snow. Take care.

Dry clothing is important in treating hypothermia. Logic will tell you that heat rises from the fire in the direction dictated by the wind. This is the best location to spread clothing that needs to be dried. Clothes racks can be made from propped poles, loose branches, or makeshift clotheslines. Clothing can be propped up, laid over or threaded onto your support. Remove articles from the heat as soon as they are dry. Dry items scorch and burn quickly. See diagrams.

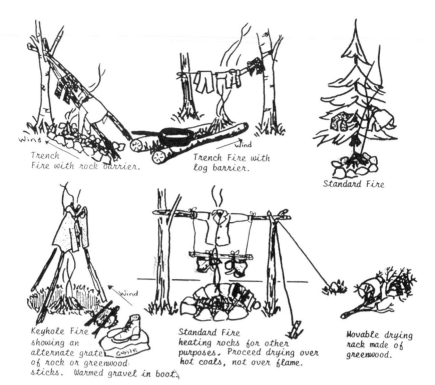

Trench Fire with rock barrier.

Trench Fire with log barrier.

Standard Fire

Keyhole Fire showing an alternate grate of rock or greenwood sticks. Warmed gravel in boot.

Standard Fire heating rocks for other purposes. Proceed drying over hot coals, not over flame.

Movable drying rack made of greenwood.

Clothes Racks:
– Hang clothes where heat rises from the fire (wind direction).
– Hang or spread clothes to single thickness.
– Thread clothes onto poles or rope through sleeves, belt loops, button holes etc.
– Smooth clothes on hot rocks.
– Fill boots, mitts, socks, pockets with hot rocks, gravel or sand to aid drying.

Alternate Fires:
Standard Fire – This fire needs a reflector to direct heat and it may be hard to control in wind.
Trench Fire – This is a long slender fire built parallel to the wind direction between two controlling barriers such as rocks, greenwood logs, dry logs or a trench dug in the ground. The downwind end of the fire is a hot blaze, and coals are raked upwind in the trench for the controlled heat needed when cooking and drying. This is an excellent fire.
Keyhole Fire – This is a variation of the standard fire with the added keyhole for cooking. It is shown dug into the ground for wind protection; excellent on the prairies. It can also be made with a large rim of rocks to direct the heat upwards.
Winter Fires – Winter fires sink into the snow very quickly and therefore should initially be built on a platform of logs to get the logs blazing well before they sink down into the melting snow.

Clothes Racks and Alternate Fires

You may want a smoke fire by day and a fire to provide light by night to to attract searchers. If firewood is plentiful, you may want to keep a smoke fire burning downwind from your shelter but still close enough for monitoring during the daylight hours when searchers are apt to be on the lookout. Damp grass and wet or green leaves banked over a good bed of coals will produce smoke. At night, keep an armful or more of fine branches prepared and dry ready to be thrown onto the fire to start a flame up if you hear searchers or an airplane. Don't burn down the shelter in your panic to start the blazing beacon. Push or drag some of the night fire in front of the shelter away from the immediate vicinity and use this hotbed of coals to initiate the flare up with the fine branches. Continue to feed this secondary fire for as long as you want the light beacon. You can see the importance of maintaining a large supply of firewood if at all possible.

Staying Dry

In the wilderness it is difficult to stay dry. Always consider what you are doing and how it affects your ability to stay dry. Remember, wet clothing takes enormous quantities of heat from your skin and this reduces your energy 25 times faster than if you are wearing dry clothing.

On the Trail

When stopping for rest periods, or setting up camp, don't brush up against wet undergrowth, kick through wet grass, get unnecessarily snowy, sit on damp surfaces, put your gear down on wet surfaces, or sit directly on the snow. Always control you trouser cuffs to prevent them from acting like a wick in drawing up moisture. Hang your gear in low branches, or where there is drainage and reduced moisture. Use your rain gear *before* you get wet. Use your sit-upon for protection against ground moisture for *all* rest periods. At times of high activity remember to reduce excess clothing and lower your rate of work to a level which does not produce perspiration.

In a Vehicle

To prevent moisture build-up caused by breathing in this confined area, open a window on the downwind side of the vehicle just a crack and burn a candle at floor level. The more people in the car, the bigger the ventilation outlet must be. If running the car from time to time, be sure the exhaust pipe of the car is free to discharge fumes and not covered by drifting snow or wet undergrowth. From time to time, with the engine shut off, open a car door to exchange moisture laden air for freshly oxygenated air. This also keeps the door from becoming blocked by drifting snow, in case a swift exit is needed to attract searchers. Restrict the interior space in the car to having just enough room for the occupants so there are fewer cold air pockets where condensation can take place, i.e., block off the back area in a station wagon or the unused seats in a car; crushed balls of newspaper are effective for this.

In a Tent

Erect the tent with the door away from the wind. Keep the tent flap free for ventilation. Exchange the air in the tent from time to time for fresh air, to remove moisture laden air. Add heat to help evaporate excess moisture in the tent. Some build-up of moist, heated air assists the hypothermia victim to breathe, so only be concerned with excess moisture if you are getting damp from it. If ice or frost forms on the inside of the roof, crack or scrape it off, entrapping the particles as they fall for easy removal before it melts or gets underfoot. Try to further insulate the outside roof of the tent with boughs or a spare ground sheet to assist in ice prevention. Snow can be thrown over the boughs for further insulation.

In the Campsite

Watch for problems of melting snow and rain run-off giving way to mud. In the most used areas of ground in front of the tent, around the fire and any paths commonly used in the area, if you have the energy, spread branches, boughs, small trees or anything that will make a matting to walk on. This matting of branches will further insulate you from the coldness of the ground.

Organize something for the person on fire duty and the person attending to the hypothermia victims to sit on. It should insulate them from the cold, keep them dry and give them support to rest at their job. Organize the best insulation and moisture barrier possible for resting persons under cover of the shelter. Here they will breathe the warmest air and in turn add warmed, moistened air for the victims to breathe.

Conclusions and Recommendations

If you have started your trip with the effective planning suggested in Chapter Five, you should be able to protect yourself from an unexpected delay in the wilderness that makes you vulnerable to hypothermia.

The theory explained in Chapter Six regarding choosing a campsite, making a shelter and a fire, and staying dry, will help you cope with an emergency. Environmental conditions will be unique with each trip. Each individual will need to utilize common sense when applying this knowledge. Good luck!.

Conclusion

It is hoped that you have come to recognize that prevention of hypothermia through understanding and planning is your first line of defense against this illness. Hypothermia is insidious in its onset. It creeps up on you and presents itself as a full blown problem all too quickly if you are not watching for it. Even when prepared, hypothermia is alarming and difficult to treat unless its symptoms are recognized early and relief is found quickly.

In addition to memorizing the *Basic Rules For Treatment Of Hypothermia*, you should try to retain the following phrases taken from Chapter Two's section, Understanding Hypothermia. Understanding this theory is the basis for good judgement in decision-making regarding hypothermia.

- Use total body energy wisely.
- Work with body physiology and its defense mechanisms against cold.
- Insulate against body heat loss caused by radiation, conduction, convection and evaporation.
- Recognize weather conditions that induce hypothermia: moisture, wind and cold.

With the information found in this book it is quite obvious which actions saved the two boys in the story *The Silent Killer*. Reread the story and you will notice the little details that foretell of trouble. These are all details you must consider to achieve good planning for your next trip to the wilderness.

If further information is desired on hypothermia, cold weather accidents or complications associated with hypothermia, consult reference books on the subject and the medical profession. The first aid knowledge to treat frostbite and other complications of a wilderness experience are beyond the realm of this introductory guide to hypothermia.

Appendix A

Quick List
for Treatment of Hypothermia

Appendix A	*Quick List for Treatment of Hypothermia*
Basic Rules of Treatment	Treating Early Warning Signs Ambulatory Treatment
Be Gentle	Urge the victim onward but do not rush.
Be Quick	Make your decisions for assisting victim and do it. Inactivity is chilling, you have one hour.
Rest	Carry victim's pack, support him or her, stop often for short rests, then go on.
Anti-Wind	Cover victim with gear or plastic sheeting.
Anti-Rain	Cover victim with rain gear or plastic sheeting.
Anti-Cold	Cover victim with survival blanket, extra clothes and/or sleeping bag worn as a cloak.
Wet Clothing	Remove wet clothes and replace with dry.
Insulation	Wear hat, hands and face protection and whatever you have that still allows mobility.
Applying Warmth	Not needed as long as victim is moving. The activity will keep the victim warm.
Giving Drink	Give the victim sweet drinks. No coffee or alcohol. Warm drinks are more supportive.
Giving Food	Give the victim food with easy to digest high carbohydrates. Warm soup, candy. No cigarettes.

in the Field – *Read Across Both Pages* – *Appendix A continued*	
Treating Mild Hypothermia	Treating Profound Hypothermia
in a temporary campsite	in wilderness conditions
Move, lift, insulate victim with care. Use a supportive voice.	Use extreme care in moving, etc. Use a stretcher if possible.
Insulate victim and start warming as quickly as possible. Organize camp and fire, to treat whole group quickly.	
The victim should rest in a horizontal position with feet raised. Monitor the victim. Don't forget insulated support for monitor to rest. Inside a shelter, rest area for all. Slight case – may wish to sit up (less cold conduction).	
The victim must be in a shelter away from the wind so the air being breathed can be warmed and moistened by all.	
Victim must have shelter with a moisture barrier. Dry all wet clothes. Work at keeping group, shelter and site dry.	
Use survival blanket. Place extra insulation on and under victim. Warm air in shelter. Insulation should be placed under every group member.	
Every group member must change wet clothing, victim first, or wrap in plastic/rain gear against evaporation until clothes can be dried. *Get into dry clothing!* Keep from perspiring!	
Insulate under, around and over victim. Use hat and mitts. Keep insulation dry. Keep socks dry.	
Heat shelter. Apply heat to body core and all body if you can, but never to frozen tissue.	Apply *only* to body core – the head, neck, armpits, and groin. Heat shelter.
Give the victim lukewarm sweet water. No coffee, strong tea or alcohol.	Nothing to drink – the victim can't swallow.
Give the victim high carbohydrates, no fat or protein. Increase amounts given as tolerated.	Nothing.

Appendix B

Useful Emergency Items

In the event of an emergency, everything you and the group have with you, becomes part of your emergency gear. These items may be useful in keeping you on the move toward safety thus avoiding hypothermia, while other items may be involved directly with treating the illness. For this reason the items have been divided into two groups: Useful items for those on foot in the wilderness, and outfitting your vehicle for emergencies.

Useful Items for Those on Foot in the Wilderness

The nature of the trip, the ultimate distance from civilization and the seasonal environment to be encountered, will determine your choice of gear. Items you carry on your person have been placed there based on convenience and the importance of the item. The rest you must carry on your back. Choose what you take carefully!

The amount of gear in your pack will be limited to the weight and bulk of equipment you are physically capable of carrying. The maximum limit of pack weight for those who are strong and fit, is equal to one fifth of their body weight. If you are of average fitness, if the trail is difficult or you wish to be comfortable on the trail, you should certainly carry less than this maximum weight. Perhaps as low as half this weight if you are new to carrying a pack.

Many items can be shared in a group. For this reason, a larger variety of equipment can be carried if there are hikers in the group sharing common items such as a stove, axe, tent or complete first aid kit. This also suggests there is more support and safety available with more people in the group; provided all are of similar ability and stamina and the size of the group does not become unmanageable.

Items To Carry On Your Person	
Basic Clothing:	**Layered Clothing** that opens down the front for easy ventilation. Suitable, comfortable underwear and socks.
	Good Boots treated to resist moisture.
	Suitable Hat for the season.
	Leather Belt for mending gear, first aid, as a rope etc.
	Neckerchief which can be carried in your pocket or pack for a sling or holding a dressing, facial protection from cold, wind, and dust, or sweat band.
In Your Pockets:	**Personal Identification** and names to contact in an emergency.
	Pocket Knife with extra features; i.e., hole punch, saw, scissors, screwdriver etc. Perhaps add a sheath knife on your belt for heavier work.
	Wooden Matches in a moisture proof container.
	Zippo Lighter: Freshly filled to work in cold weather.
	Safety Pins of varying sizes but mostly large.
	Bead Whistle: The sound is identified with distress, calling is tiring and voices don't always carry well.
	Length Of Stout String for an extra shoe lace, gear repair, light rope etc.
	Handkerchief: A cloth hanky can take over when the Kleenex runs out.
	Gorp/Candies or other high energy food.
	Compass: There should be at least two compasses in the group, in the event you split the group and send the faster ones on for assistance.
	Pocket First Aid Kit for your supply of sun screen, insect repellent, personal medications and treatment of small injuries. Include some high energy tablets, money and quarters for phone calls at unattended outdoor phones. This Kit could also be kept in your pack, with only timely items in your pockets.
	Water Bottle: Use the 1/2 litre size, as the one litre size is too heavy to carry when full. This could also be carried in a readily accessible pocket of your pack.

Items To Carry In Your Pack	
Clothing:	**Protective Clothing** against moisture, wind and cold. Good Quality rain gear, or effective, insulating winter clothing, depending on the season. **Extra Clothing Changes** according to need. **Extra Jacket** for times of reduced activity. **Extra Socks**: Change your socks often. Perspiration damp socks allow your feet to get cold. **Mitts, Neck Tube or Scarf, and Tuque**: The tuque is worn for cold weather sleeping as well. **Gaiters** to control pant cuffs in rain and snow.
Personal Items:	**Personal Kit**: comb, soap, toothbrush etc. and towel. A mirror is also useful for reflecting sunlight signals. **Plate or Bowl, Cup and Cutlery** if cooking meals. **Flashlight** and extra batteries. **Matches** in a waterproof container; a second supply. **Survival Blanket**: This could also be shared gear, but it is best if each hiker has his or her own. **Insulite Sit-Upon** for insulation and moisture barrier when sitting, or resting. Three or four could be placed side by side for treating the victim of an emergency. **Large Plastic Garbage Bag/s** are very useful against moisture and wind either used as a groundsheet or pulled down over your outer clothing with holes cut for your arms and head. They are also useful for keeping starter firewood dry, for protecting equipment exposed to rain or snow, and for blocking wind, rain or snow in the the walls or roof of shelter. **Toilet Paper and Kleenex** **Sun Glasses** **Sleeping Equipment** if involved with an overnight trip. A sleeping bag of suitable weight for the environment inner liner. It is easier to dry a liner that is damp with perspiration, than to dry a moist sleeping bag. A "mattress" such as Insulite acts as a moisture barrier and insulation under the sleeping bag.
Shared Items:	**Adequate Food** for the group *plus* a little extra. **Pots and Cooking Utensils** suitable to the menu.

Items To Carry In Your Pack *continued*	
Shared Items *continued:*	**Lightweight Stove** and extra fuel. **Fire Starter** cubes or paste. Extra matches. **Maps**: Two sets in case the group must split up for help. **Axe, Saw or Garrotte Saw**: A garrotte is a wire saw saw with handles on either end, designed for lightweight backpacking. **Complete First Aid Kit** to treat cuts, burns, bites, slivers, fever, pain, sprains, infections, fractures and frostbite. **Water Purifying Kit** and instructions. Two kits in case the group must split to go for help. **Tent/s** to house all hikers, if involved in an overnight trip. For day trips some type of shelter should be planned such as a tent or large sheet of plastic, or survival blanket depending on the season. **Tools** suitable for repairing your equipment like the stove, or cross country skis and ski harness. **Extra Snow Seal** for moisture proofing boots if you are involved with extended hiking – over many days. **Waxes, Spare Ski Tip, Bale and Basket** if you are involved in cross country skiing. **Note Paper and Pencil** **Lightweight Rope and Food Bag** for suspending the food cache high in a tree overnight for safety from animals. A simple food bag can be made with a net onion sack for strength, suspended inside a sealed large plastic garbage bag, for retaining food aromas. **Extra Lightweight Ropes**

As can be seen, the mountain of gear that can be taken seems endless. You must plan carefully to include the most important items possible within weight limits that relate to the type of trip planned and the number of people involved.

Outfitting Your Vehicle For Emergencies

Service your car before going on the highway to be sure that all systems are functioning properly and the air pressure is correct in the tires. A clean car with a gleaming exterior is more visible on the highway than a dirty car. Make up a collection of emergency gear. Keep some of the items in the glove compartment. Larger items and a gym bag containing the rest of the smaller items, can be stowed elsewhere in your vehicle.

This may look like a lot of gear, but it is surprising how compact it can be made. Some items are the same as suggested for hiking. One kit of duplicated items, carried in the vehicle, then transferred to your pack for the outing, will serve both purposes if organized suitably.

Items To Carry In Your Vehicle	
Vehicle Related Equipment:	**Spare Tire** in good condition and properly inflated.
	Jack and Lug Wrench.
	Spare Fuses for various vehicle systems.
	Booster Cables
	Tow Rope
	Tire Chains and a Bag Of Sand if applicable
	Spare Antifreeze for windshield wipers.
	Warning Devices such as road markers for day or night.
	Tools: A small assortment of tools such as pliers, screwdriver and wrenches. Work gloves for cold days.
	Ice Scraper and Snow Brush if applicable.
Other Emergency Equipment:	**Registration and Insurance Papers**
	Flashlight: Check the flashlight and spare batteries from time to time.
	High Calorie, Long-life Nutrients such as Dextra-sol.
	Note Paper and Pencil.
	Pocket Knife.
	Quarters for pay phone calls.
	Phone Numbers for people or companies to be called in the event of an emergency.
	Road Maps of the area you intend to travel.
	Fire Extinguisher suitable for use with gasoline.

Items to Carry in Your Car (continued)	
	Empty Can in which to carry gasoline, water or melt snow.
	First Aid Kit including water purifying kit. This can be the same one you take hiking.
	Small compact Shovel
	Wooden Matches in a moistureproof container. **Inflammable Paste or Cubes** to make a fire start.
	Metal Can or Dish for candle holder and candles, to warm the interior of the car while waiting for help.
	Car Blanket
	Survival Blanket (purchase at a hostel shop).
	Newspaper for fire centre, wrapping around you for warmth or crumpling in balls to fill excess interior space within the vehicle to limit the area requiring heat.
	Toilet Paper
	Saw or Axe
	Sheet of Plastic to windproof the interior of the vehicle in the event of broken windows. A tarpaulin may also be used.
	White Cloth or Shirt to wear if you are working on the highway at night.
	Brightly Colored Cloth to tie to the radio antenna or raise above the vehicle to attract rescuers.
Short Term Emergency Equipment:	**Warm Protective Clothing** suitable for the trip, including boots, mitts, and facial protection.
	High Calorie Food: Arrange to carry some food suitable for consumption in the vehicle, with sufficient for a light meal and snacks for everyone.
	Thermos of Water, suitable for a hot drink or other non-alcoholic beverage, sufficient for each person in the group to have at least a 1/2 litre of fluid each. Do not consume alcohol when threatened with cold or an emergency.

Again, the nature of the trip, its distance from civilization and highway assistance, and the seasonal dangers that could be encountered all have a bearing on what gear will be chosen when planning the trip.

References

Boy Scouts of Canada: Calgary Region. *21st Century Approach to Camping*. Calgary: Boy Scouts of Canada: Calgary Region, 1973.

Canada Indian and Eskimo Affairs Program: Employment and Related Services. *Northern Survival*. Ottawa: Information Canada, 1972.

Collins, K.J., *Hypothermia The Facts*. Oxford: Oxford University Press, 1983.

Forgey, W. *Death By Exposure – Hypothermia*. Merrillville: ICS Books Inc., 1985.

Kahn, Frederick H., and B.R. Visscher. "Water Disinfection In The Wilderness." *West Journal of Medicine* 122 (1975): 450–453.

Kochanski, Mors L., *Northern Bush Craft*. Edmonton: Lone Pine Publishing, 1987.

Pozos, Robert S., and David O. Born. *Hypothermia*. Piscataway: New Century Publishers Inc., 1982.

Thompson, Lyn. "Lightweight Stove Characteristics." Paper presented to Boy Scouts Canada – Calgary Region, Calgary, 1978.

Wilkerson, James A., Cameron C. Bangs, John S. Hayward, with the assistance of Mark S. Tuttle. *Hypothermia, Frostbite and Other Cold Injuries*. Vancouver: Douglas and McIntyre Ltd., 1986.